aaliyah

more than a woman

christopher
john farley

POCKET BOOKS
new york london toronto sydney singapore

An *Original* Publication of POCKET BOOKS

POCKET BOOKS, a division of Simon & Schuster, Inc.
1230 Avenue of the Americas, New York, NY 10020

ISBN: 0-7434-5140-6

First MTV Books/Pocket Books printing December 2001

10 9 8 7 6 5 4 3 2 1

For information regarding special discounts for bulk purchases, please contact Simon & Schuster Special Sales at 1-800-456-6798 or business@simonandschuster.com

Cover design by Youri Lenquette/Retna

Printed in the U.S.A.

MORE THAN A WOMAN

In Arabic, the name Aaliyah means "the highest, most exalted one; the best." And while Aaliyah was not quite a household name, to true music fans her prodigious gifts were well known. When she died in a tragic accident at the early age of 22, her loss was deeply felt. Aaliyah was one of a handful of artists pushing the boundaries of popular music and brought a whole new sonic palette to hip-hop and soul. She had street credibility and mainstream appeal; she was smart, sexy, and sensitive and a canny businesswoman; she was a prodigy who grew up before our eyes into a true adult superstar.

Featuring new interviews with Aaliyah's family and friends, tributes from superstars such as Beyoncé Knowles of Destiny's Child, and new information about the crash investigation, *MORE THAN A WOMAN* is the first book to examine the young diva's brief but unforgettable life.

"Aaliyah had the ear and she had the voice. She knew how to pick a song and she knew how to make it hot."

—Missy Elliott

"She was exquisitely beautiful and full of light and love. As an artist she was only getting better and better."

—Michael Rymer, director of *The Queen of the Damned*

"Aaliyah inspired me to keep on a musical path. She inspired me because she always experimented and tried new things. She inspired me in her passing too because, as sad as it was, it helped teach me to live life to the fullest and appreciate every day."

—Alicia Keys

For Mom, Dad, Anthony, Felipe, Jonathan, Lia, and Sharon

contents

introduction

> I think what we've got to learn out of this is to appreciate each other while we're here on earth. I love you Aaliyah, and you're forever missed.
>
> —Missy "Misdemeanor" Elliott

The month after 22-year-old hip-hop/soul singer Aaliyah was killed in a plane crash in the Bahamas, more than 5,000 people were murdered in the September 11th terrorist attacks. In the face of such tragedy, who is Aaliyah? Tragedies happen every day and, in a time of terror and heartbreak, they are likely to happen more often. What is the life of one promising young singer compared to the prematurely extinguished existences of the bond traders and window washers and security people who worked at the World Trade Center everyday? What is her one life balanced against the lives of the hundreds of firemen and police officers who gave their lives in an effort to help pull some of the victims from the conflagration? Who is Aaliyah in the face of all that?

I work as the music critic for *TIME* magazine. I talked to Aaliyah a few months before her death. I attended a small party she threw in a restaurant in New York City to celebrate the release of her third and final album, *Aaliyah*, and, the next day, I sat down and talked to her one-on-one. I found her to be gracious and eloquent, alluring and slightly mysterious, youthful and yet possessing a smooth solemnity that would be the envy of musicians twice her age. "I think my style is street but sweet," Aaliyah told me. I thought her album, *Aaliyah*, was the best R&B album of 2001. I also thought Aaliyah herself was the most promising young singer around. In a pop world ruled by Britney Spears and 'NSync, Mandy Moore and Jessica Simpson, Aaliyah was making smart, sophisticated music that was still cool to dance to. She was a siren of subtlety, and she had a polished charm that went way deeper than ordinary pop music. She was a fine dancer and she was just branching out into acting. Aaliyah told me then: "I was trained to do it all." Weeks later, when I heard the news about her death, I felt a numbing melancholy which, even as I write this, I have been unable to completely shake. I can still remember her soft smile, her dark eyes, the sheen off her long black hair, her light glide as she walked, her gentle laugh. I remember it all as clearly as the last time I saw Kurt Cobain, dressed in a faded green cardigan and holding his baby, Frances Bean, in his arms after a concert. I can remember that last image of Aaliyah as clearly as the last time I saw Tupac Shakur, filing into an MTV party with a squadron of his boys, he and his entire posse dressed in all white.

Singers die, and sometimes they die young. They have done so before, and, sadly, inevitably, they will do so again. Often they die in plane crashes. The great soul singer Otis Redding died at the age of 26 in a plane crash in Lake Monoma, near Madison, Wisconsin, in 1967. Country singer Patsy Cline died at the age of 30 in a plane crash in Camden, Tennessee in 1963. Bandleader Glenn Miller, just 40 years old, disappeared over the English Channel in 1944, perhaps shot down by German fighters. Buddy Holly, 22; J.P. "Big Bopper" Richardson, 28; and Ritchie Valens, 17, perished in a plane accident near Clear Lake, Iowa in 1959. They called that plane crash "The Day the Music Died."

Musicians are perhaps more vulnerable to air disasters because they are always traveling. They are often on the move, from one gig to another; they are often traveling quickly and on the cheap. Such is the nature of touring, especially for young, up-and-coming acts that are just making their marks on the world of entertainment. When you're a professional athlete, even a rookie, you're part of a team and you're traveling in style; when you're a movie star, even a novice one, whatever movie you're shooting is probably only going to have a handful of locations. Musicians may play several cities a week, hundreds of gigs a year. Their shows are often in small towns and out-of-the-way places that require small planes to fly into small airports. It opens their lives up to tragedy.

When a musician dies, and the music they had yet to make dies with them, something else is born. The blues, and the suffering associated with them, are at the heart of American music; when a musician meets a tragic end, it brings out the bluesy core of the music. When we hear the music again, in the wake of catastrophe, the work suddenly seems richer, deeper, sadder. Kurt Cobain. Tupac Shakur. Selena. Jimi Hendrix. Jim Morrison. They all died young. Because of that, their music seems forever young as well, eternally bursting with an empathetic melancholy, and a mordantly attractive cool. I was in the audience when Kurt Cobain sang his punkish version of Leadbelly's blues classic "Where Did You Sleep Last Night?" It was powerful then, but when I listened to it again after Kurt's death, it had a new, sad and sublime majesty. Tragedy brings with it a kind of grandness. In 1997, I had set up a lunchtime interview with the rapper The Notorious B.I.G. to talk to him about his forthcoming album. A few days later he was murdered in Los Angeles; the day of our appointment turned out to be the day of his funeral. His album, *Life After Death,* took on new resonance.

And now Aaliyah is another pop tragedy. But should we care about the death of musicians? Should we listen closely for the blue echo of Aaliyah's voice given the disastrous din of other tragedies we hear all around? The rapper Jay-Z, on a New York City radio interview, expressed the thought that Aaliyah's death, for him, felt like a precursor to the World Trade Center disaster. One catastrophe was intimate, the other global: both were hard to take. But was he overstating the case? What larger meaning can we really draw from individual fatalities? In Thornton Wilder's classic novel *The Bridge of San Luis Rey* he writes about a simple monk named Brother Juniper who is witness to an inexplicable tragedy: he sees five people fall to their deaths after a rope bridge they are crossing suddenly breaks. He wonders: Why those people? Why those five? What is the answer to the riddle of tragedy?

In the end there is one answer: simply by caring, by connecting emotionally to such events, we give them meaning. In other words, the search for meaning can itself be meaningless. We create the meaning ourselves; what we take from such experiences is entirely in our own hands. Many Americans, outside of members of the Hispanic community and residents of Texas, had never even heard of Selena before she died. The mourning of her fans drew the attention of others and Hollywood besides; the passion of her core group of fans gave her passing impact and import. At the conclusion of *The Bridge of San Luis Rey,* Wilder writes, "Soon we shall die and all the memory of those five will have left the earth, and we ourselves shall be loved for awhile and forgotten. But the love will have been enough; all those impulses of love return to the love that made them. Even memory is not necessary for love. There is a land of the living and a land of the dead and the bridge is love, the only survival, the only meaning."

Music is worth celebrating. Loss is worth remembering. We fight disaster with remembrance, cataloging the things that gave us joy, the art that made life worth living, and the artists that created it. Artists give us the metaphors, the emotions, the lyrics, the melodies, and the rhythms that help us make some sense of the rest of the world's struggles. The week after the terrorist attacks in New York and Washington, several different groups of artists announced that they planned to record a tribute song to benefit the survivors, and a huge musical telethon was broadcast on all the major networks simultaneously. When calamity strikes, music is there to console, to uplift, and to rejuvenate.

When we investigate the death of an artist, and the life of that artist as well, it's not just about the artist, it's about all that they represent. Performers like Bob Marley and Bob Dylan, Nirvana and Lauryn Hill, evoke in their works and lives things specific and universal, they are both associated with certain decades and with something timeless. When Aaliyah went down in that plane in the Bahamas, more than eight people died with her: Some small part of every one of her fans also crashed with her. Can we ever get what we lost back?

The day of the World Trade Center attack, I was in the Time & Life building in midtown Manhattan. I could see the smoke from the ruined twin towers spiraling into what had been a clear blue sky. I thought then, as I think now, that in the face of catastrophe we need heroes. We need legends. We need people who live lives of such richness and intensity and grace that, even when they pass away, we are moved to tell their stories again and again, and the tales grow in the telling. In such a way, and with such stories, we lay a foundation in our culture that can never be shattered, and we offer up to every person the chance of immortality, a life that can last longer than concrete and steel, if they simply dare to achieve greatness. These legends of our own making can be firefighters or teachers, scientists or artists; they are, of course, not all equivalent, but they are all important. It's not about hero worship, it's about every single person having the chance to be the next Aaliyah or the next icon or the next superstar if they're willing to take the chances and make the sacrifices.

So this book is about one ordinary woman who I think led an extraordinary life. She died young, but she was also old beyond her years. For the most part, she didn't write her own hit songs, but the way she performed them broke new ground. I don't think this is a book about tragedy or loss, I think it's a work about remembrance and tribute. The filmmaker Woody Allen, in the movie *Another Woman,* once posed the question, "Is a memory something you have or something you've lost?" If it is the former, we'll always have John Lennon. We'll always have Tupac. We'll always have Jimi and Biggie, Kurt and Selena. And we'll always have Aaliyah.

1 | rock the boat

She was always a hard worker. Always. That was just her.

—TIMBALAND, AALIYAH'S LONGTIME PRODUCER

The weather said nothing.

It was another perfect day on Abaco, a tiny island in the Bahamas about 200 miles northeast of Miami. The weather was warm, the sky was smiling and so was Aaliyah. She had every reason to be happy. The young singer's new album, the self-titled *Aaliyah,* was a hit. It had debuted high on the *Billboard* charts and had received rave reviews from the likes of *TIME, Spin,* and *Vibe* magazines. The veteran music publication *Rolling Stone* had given the new CD four stars, declaring that "on *Aaliyah,* a near-flawless declaration of strength and independence, she ups the ante for herself and her contemporaries—as well as her musical heroes. *Aaliyah* is *Control, Velvet Rope,* and *Jagged Little Pill* all rolled into one."

Aaliyah had other reasons to be happy as well. Recently, she had secretly become engaged to Damon Dash, the co-CEO of Roc-a-Fella records, a leading hip-hop label and the home to Jay-Z and a number of other top rappers. The pair had refused to comment on their relationship to the press, but it was an open secret among their friends and close fans. Dash and Aaliyah were often seen out on the town, sometimes in Harlem, sometimes in the Hamptons, always smiling, laughing, clearly enjoying one another's company. Their engagement wasn't formal—few things are in the hip-hop world—but Dash planned on marrying his new sweetheart as soon as time opened up in her busy schedule for them to do it up right. Meanwhile, they were living the life, having a good time: the newest prince and princess of hip-hop nightlife.

Aaliyah's schedule, however, was punishing. She had long ago set her sights on being a total entertainer—a star of both concert stages and movie screens—and the commitment required sacrifice. She was now working hard to make sure her new album had a long shelf life and had come to the Bahamas to film a video for her latest single, a song titled "Rock the Boat." Filming for the video kicked off in Miami on August 22nd, and it required some difficult underwater shots. After that part of the shoot, Aaliyah and about a dozen of her associates flew down to the Bahamas to complete the project.

It was a loose-knit, jovial group. Everybody was working hard, but everyone was having a good time. Gina Smith, 30, born in Fort Worth, Texas but living in New Jersey, had recently come on board Team Aaliyah as product manager for Aaliyah's label, Blackground Records. Aaliyah had called Smith herself when she got the job, which entailed living, breathing, and sleeping Aaliyah's music and making sure it got a deserving amount of publicity from the press and attention from radio stations. Smith worked in New York, but never lost her southern courtliness.

Then there was Eric Foreman, 29, of Hollywood, who was Aaliyah's hairstylist. He was known as a funny man, the kind of guy that kept everybody laughing; the kind of guy who, one wild night in Atlanta, climbed up on stage at a club and performed his own all-in-fun, improptu strip tease that was, by one report, far more entertaining that anything else on stage that evening.

There was also makeup artist Christopher Maldonado, 32, of New York. He wasn't the regular makeup guy, but he was best friends with Aaliyah's makeup artist who, while tied up in Europe with Macy Gray, had dispatched his pal Maldonado to fill his slot. Maldonado was the opposite of Foreman: He was laid back and calm, always collected, never excited, taking life as it comes. He liked to party as much as the next guy, but he was always cool about it.

Protecting Aaliyah was her 6-foot 8-inch, 300-pound bodyguard Scott Gallin, 41, of Pompano Beach, Florida. Gallin was a big guy, but was, by all accounts, a friendly and caring one as well. He was a divorced dad who had custody of his 15-year-old son, Lyle, to whom he was devoted. He had worked as a bouncer in various joints around South Florida, but he was an aspiring actor as well, and had appeared in small roles in the movies *Any Given Sunday* and *Holy Man.* As a bodyguard he was in high demand—Ricky Martin, Madonna, and Rosie O'Donnell had used his services in the past. He was the kind of full-service, beyond-the-call-of-duty bodyguard who, if the client was out of town, would call up the client's spouse, just to make sure they were okay. Right now he was totally focused on his current employer, Aaliyah. Nothing bad would happen to her as long as he could help it.

So with that cast of characters, the shoot was bound to be a good time. What's not to enjoy about being in the Bahamas on a beautiful day? What's not to love about dancing on a 72-foot catamaran as it glides through clear Caribbean waters? You can feel the joy when you see scenes of the video: Aaliyah's on a beach, the ocean stretched out behind her; Aaliyah wearing a sexy red top, and dancing slyly, suggestively, playfully before the cameras. "It was a fun shoot," said Annie Russell, a local taxi operator who organized a squad of drivers to assist the video crew. "Everybody in that group was getting along fine, like they loved one another." The first day Aaliyah arrived, she and Gallin asked Russell where they could rent some motorscooters. Clearly work and play were going to mix on this trip.

The video was helmed by one of the best directors in the business: Hype Williams. When you wanted a hit video, when you wanted a clip that the suburbs would groove to but the streets would respect, you signed up Hype. In the past, Williams had worked with Busta Rhymes, the Notorious B.I.G., and Missy "Misdemeanor" Elliott. That video with Missy Elliott in the puffy costume? ("Supa Dupa Fly [The Rain]" if you don't know). That's Hype. That video with Sean "P. Diddy" Combs in the shiny suit? ("Been Around the World"). That's Hype.

Work started that day around 10 A.M. The video went off like any other. Lots of stops and starts. Lots of makeup touch-ups. Lots of adjustments to the lighting. Aaliyah never complained. That wasn't her style. "Lots of people in this business are hard to work with," says one publicist who worked with Aaliyah. "She's always professional. She's always, what do you need me to do, how can I help. She never takes a star trip. She's an angel. She's like an angel sent down to earth." That day, Aaliyah was in nearly all of the shots: after all, it was her video. But instead of retiring to her cabin after her scene, she would stay and watch the other shots, observing the process and supporting everyone else.

Around 2 P.M. everyone broke for lunch. Around 5 P.M. they were all done. Aaliyah washed off her makeup and prepared to leave. She signed a few autographs and then got into a cab. "Bye! See you all later!" she cheerfully called out to Russell and a few of the others who had come to say their farewells.

And why shouldn't she have been happy? She had work to do, but it was work she loved. She had commitments to keep back in the States, but she was looking forward to keeping them. She had cool music in the works, including a collaboration with hip-hop/folk star Beck called "I Am Music" that her longtime creative partner, Timbaland, was producing. Her movie career was taking off. She had recently finished filming *The Queen of the Damned,* a movie based on the Anne Rice novel. The big screen adaptation starred Aaliyah as the title character, an ancient—but eternally youthful—vampire. She had also signed on to star in not just one, but two sequels to the action franchise *The Matrix.* She was set to take some martial arts training and then fly down to Australia to begin filming.

But even before that she had a date with MTV.

She was going to be a presenter at the upcoming MTV Video Music Awards. It was the party everyone wanted to be at—U2, OutKast, No Doubt, Nelly, Janet Jackson, they were all scheduled to be there. Aaliyah just wanted to get back to Florida and then New York City so she could hook up with Dash, chill for a little bit, and then start doing the things she needed to do. The first order of business, however, was to get off Abaco and out of the Bahamas. She'd had a good time, but now it was time to roll.

Aaliyah, along with Maldonado, Smith, Foreman, Gallin, three other passengers, and the pilot, Luis Morales III, boarded a twin-engine Cessna 402B.

The plane rolled down the runway.

It was Saturday, August 25, 2001.

It was a warm day. The sky was smiling.

Disaster was moments away.

The weather said nothing.

2 | the (very) early years

One day we will be together again . . . We will always love you.

—Janet Jackson on Aaliyah

Detroit, Michigan, is the kind of place that's large enough to have the toughness of a big city but small enough to have some of the everybody-knows-everybody affability of a small town.

That's partly why Detroit has long been known as a spawning ground for new sounds. In 1959, Berry Gordy renovated a two-story house on 2648 West Grand Boulevard and put these words over the entrance: "Hitsville U.S.A." Motown Records, home to Stevie Wonder, Marvin Gaye, The Supremes and many other top music acts, was born. Detroit, in the '60s, became the capital of youth music, with singers and songwriters, girl groups and instrumentalists, all flocking there to work with Gordy and his stable of hot acts: the Temptations, the Four Tops, and many others. When cities produce sounds or scenes, they are often fleeting trends, material for a few newspaper lifestyle stories and little more. The music that Motown made in the '60s and '70s not only helped define American pop culture during those decades, it still continues to do so today. Songs like Marvin Gaye's "What's Going On," albums like Stevie Wonder's *Songs in the Key of Life,* and timeless performances such as Diana Ross and the Supremes' rendition of "Stop! In the Name of Love" set a high standard for all the pop music that followed. Contemporary hip-hoppers still borrow samples from the Motown catalog, and contemporary pop groups, from TLC to Destiny's Child, continue to imitate some of the glamorous style of the Motown era.

Detroit also produced other significant musical artists. Michael Jackson (who started on Motown), Janet Jackson, and the entire Jackson clan are from Gary, Indiana, which is about a four-hour car trip away. The great soul singer Aretha Franklin hails from Detroit, as does rocker Bob Seger. Eminem and Kid Rock are from Detroit—it's a tribute to the breadth and depth of Detroit culture that the same city that gave rise to the sophisticated sounds of Motown in the '60s also helped created the in-yo-face yowl of white boy hardcore hip-hop in the '90s.

But it was the tradition of Motown—classy but cool, mainstream and yet closely connected with African American culture—that most deeply affected the course of Aaliyah's career. Motown, in its heyday, had an "artist development program," basically a charm school for its artists to learn how to dress, to study comportment and choreography, and to learn basic etiquette. Many of Motown's artists were drawn from the middle class and, for them, artist development was simply a refresher course. Before Motown, many prominent intellectuals, including black thinkers such as Carter G. Woodson and Booker T. Washington, believed that most forms of Black music worked to erode the respectability of African American culture. Motown disproved such theories and helped lay the foundation for a new approach to marketing in American pop. Suzanne E. Smith, in her book *Dancing in the Streets: Motown and the Cultural Politics of Detroit,* writes, "[Motown] sought to produce the black music of Detroit but also to package it in such a way as to not contribute to any racist stereotypes of African American as uncouth or uncivilized. Motown marketed a product that proved that black popular culture could 'uplift the race' on a mass scale; it could be both 'of the people' and dignified."

Aaliyah Dana Haughton was also from Detroit. Her first name, a feminized version of the name Ali, means, loosely, the highest, the best, the most exalted one, in Arabic. "I try every day [to live up to it]," Aaliyah once said to *USA Weekend*. "It's a beautiful name. I'm very proud of it." She was born on January 16, 1979, in the Bedford-Stuyvesant neighborhood of Brooklyn, New York, but, at the age of four, her parents relocated to the Motor City where Aaliyah spent her formative years. Her home was loving, but a little offbeat. "When I was growing up we had every sort of pet imaginable," Aaliyah told *FHM* magazine. "From dogs, ducks, and cats to snakes and iguanas. My cousin actually had a baby alligator, but that was something I wasn't going to stroke."

That cousin, Jomo Hankerson, would go on in 2000 to become the president of Blackground Records, Aaliyah's record label, after having worked there full time for seven years. Jomo talked to me in October of 2001 about growing up with his famous relative in Detroit—before she was famous to anyone outside of the family. Jomo's father is Barry Hankerson, the man who founded Blackground; Barry is also the brother of Aaliyah's mother, Diane. Jomo, who is eight years older than Aaliyah, grew up hearing stories about Aaliyah and her brother, Rashad. And Aaliyah, when she was still living in Brooklyn, used to hear stories about her cousins back in the Motor City.

The various streams of family stories all had a common source. "My grandmother [Mintis Hankerson] used to tell us about each other," says Jomo. "She would tell me about Aaliyah and Rashad, and vice versa. They were just funny stories that your grandmother tells you about the cousins you haven't met yet. Like one of them was that Aaliyah was gorgeous and she had this wonderful head of hair right out of the womb."

Jomo says his extended family has always been close: "Our grandmother, she was a housewife, and my grandfather worked for the transit authority in New York City and owned a cleaners and a tailor shop at different points in his life and also drove a cab. At any point he had two or three jobs or endeavors going on." The hard work required strong support and the family drew together as a result. Said Jomo: "So there was a very strong 'family first' ethic from my grandparents and that went on to my Aunt Diane and to my dad and they continued that legacy on. Family always came first and it was us against the world."

When Aaliyah and her family moved to Detroit, Jomo and his family went over to welcome them to town to let them know that they would be there for support, if any was needed. The men of the family—Jomo's father, Barry, and Aaliyah's father, Michael—quickly began to formulate joint business ventures. Said Jomo: "When they came to town, Uncle Mike was going to be doing some deals with my dad. At the time, my dad had a warehouse business and a food distribution business so Uncle Mike was going to work with him on those. My Aunt Diane was a teacher but she stopped teaching full time when she had children so she could be home with the kids full time. She also early on had aspirations of being a professional singer herself. She did some plays that toured nationally and that featured her as a vocalist." Jomo laughed and added, "I think she and my dad made a record a long time ago."

"Aaliyah was my best friend," Rashad told *BET* in October, 2001. "She was my everything. Growing up with her was amazing. Being her big brother, you know, like any big brother and little sister we'd always get in arguments and everything, but she was always an angel. She would come to me and say 'I'm sorry' and give me a kiss on the cheek. She was always an angel from the first day since she was born. She would run around the house and sing and it was never annoying because she had a beautiful voice."

Aaliyah, Rashad and Jomo soon grew close. "Growing up we lived about five blocks apart," said Jomo. "I used to walk them home from school sometimes when Aunt Diane couldn't get there and stuff. It was a nice middle class neighborhood on the west side of Detroit. There were a lot of upwardly mobile type people that hadn't necessarily made it yet but they were doing well. Single family homes, things like that."

Jomo said that Aaliyah's household was always full of music. Every time he went over to visit there was either a record on the player, or people were just making their own joyful noises. "Aunt Diane is an incredible singer and so she always sang around the house," said Jomo. "I remember that once Rashad and Aaliyah got to Detroit, that Aaliyah and Aunt Diane would always be around the house singing. Growing up, Aaliyah would sing the whole Whitney Houston album and the whole Luther Vandross album around the house. So music was always part of her personality. She was always a great little singer."

Aaliyah attended a Catholic school early on: Gesu Elementary, which is located on the northwest side of Detroit. "I was a pretty popular kid, but I think I was like all kids and went through that awkward stage," said Aaliyah to *New York Newsday.* "I made friends and lost friends growing up." In 1985, when she was in the first grade, she won a part in a production of *Annie* and, from that point on, she wanted to be in show business. Gesu's stage productions could be elaborate affairs—many were performed at nearby Marygrove College. Gesu productions featured children ranging in age from five to 13, but the young actors took on some adult-sized responsibilities; they not only acted, danced, and sang, they also learned how to run light and sound boards. The hours were adult-sized as well: Rehearsals lasted for three hours a day, four days a week. They were held after school, so students had to deal with a full schedule of classes at the same time that they had to accommodate having their days lengthened by rehearsals. Sometimes, the sessions were held on Saturday mornings, and sometimes they were even held on official holidays, such as Easter. In the *Annie* production, Aaliyah played one of the show's many orphans, and her part was small by any standard—just a single speaking line. But it was enough to stir something deep in her and put her on the path towards an entertainment career. "I had one measly line, but I made that one line shine," Aaliyah said to *The New York Post.* And what was the line? " 'You're gonna get the paddle,' " she said.

Instead, she got a trip to the top. After her first small role, Aaliyah went on to win other, larger roles in Gesu musicals, including productions of *42nd Street* and *Hello, Dolly.* "Aaliyah was wonderful," Suzanne McGill-Anderson told *The Detroit Free Press.* At the time, McGill-Anderson was a fifth grade teacher at Gesu who also directed plays at the school. Said McGill-Anderson: "[Aaliyah] was really easy to direct; a very positive, hard-working, and disciplined child, and we auditioned literally hundreds of kids. She was able to understand the characters and bring those characters to life."

"Entertaining is innate in me," said Aaliyah. "When I was six I was in *Annie* in school. I was very, very shy back then but going out for the play helped me come out of my shell. I loved the camaraderie of it all, the acting, the dancing, all of it at one time. It was just bliss to me. To be able to act and sing now is the fulfillment of all that I've wanted to do."

The decision was Aaliyah's, but her parents, mother Diane and father Michael, completely supported her. "When I told my parents that I wanted to embark along this path, they were with me all the way," said Aaliyah. "They're the ones who shuttled me back and forth to my vocal lessons." Pretty soon, Aaliyah's parents began to manage their daughter's fledgling career. The young singer always considered her family's close involvement one of the keys to her success. "A strong belief in God and a strong family base are important," Aaliyah said.

After a time, Aaliyah's older brother Rashad even came on board Team Aaliyah. "He's always been there for me," Aaliyah said. "So I just started introducing him to people as my creative consultant. Eventually the title just stuck. We discuss everything together, from video concepts to stagewear, and we've even started to write some songs together."

When she was eight years old Aaliyah began to make a name for herself as a vocalist outside of family get-togethers. She started to perform at school functions and talent shows around the Detroit area. She also began to land singing gigs at weddings. She was quite a sight back then: a skinny girl standing up in front of amused wedding guests and a smiling bride and groom, belting out hits by soul singers who were stars even before she was born—tunes made famous by acts like Stevie Wonder and Whitney Houston.

At age ten, she signed up to work with a vocal coach, Wendelin Peddy. Not long after Aaliyah's passing, I had a chance to talk to Peddy about her time with Aaliyah. Peddy, who worked with Aaliyah before she was signed by a record company and continued to work with her during the recording of her first two albums, got to see the young superstar's development up close, closer than anyone except members of Aaliyah's family. Says Peddy: "As a ten-year-old she knew exactly what she wanted to do. She knew she wanted to be an entertainer. She had some experience. She and her parents wanted her voice to be developed and they wanted her style to develop, so that when she sang she wouldn't seem like a copycat—what you'd hear would be all Aaliyah."

So Aaliyah began to stop by Peddy's house in Detroit periodically for sessions. The coach worked on developing Aaliyah's high, light vocals—her "head voice" as she calls it—something that would, eventually, become one of Aaliyah's trademarks. The pair also worked on developing Aaliyah's breath control and on drawing emotion from a song. Because Aaliyah was so young, she didn't always have the "emotional store" to draw upon to give a song impact. Peddy taught her to create emotion within herself, to use her imagination to help fuel a song. "She had a great voice at 10," says Peddy. "Really a voice that some adults might wish that they had. So it wasn't difficult to build on that because the voice was there."

Aaliyah also had the desire. Says Peddy: "A lot of [people] have that raw talent that can be developed into stardom. But they don't have that drive and that commitment to have longevity in the business. She had it all."

At age 10, Aaliyah also got her big break—and suffered her biggest setback. Star Search, the syndicated television show hosted by Ed McMahon, was probably the most important talent show on television at that time. Of course that's largely because, other than "It's Showtime at the Apollo," it was essentially the only talent show on television. TV talent shows are pretty much a thing of the past, partly because so many of today's hot young performers aren't about talent—they're about marketing and packaging, lip-syncing and slick production. Talent competitions tend not to judge performers on how well their press releases are written.

But Aaliyah was a young performer with an old-school outlook. She wanted to be a complete performer—she was interested in training her voice and perfecting her stage moves like Whitney Houston, Aretha Franklin, and all the other great artists she admired. So entering a television talent competition was a natural for her; it gave her a place to test her developing skills and to find out what else she had to learn. One thing she needed to work on was her musical taste. In that particular area, when she was very young, Aaliyah needed a little work—the first single she ever bought was Culture Club's 1994 novelty soul hit "Karma Chameleon"—but it quickly improved. By the time she was in her early teens, her favorite artists were ones that had proved their longevity, stars who had made it to the top long before Aaliyah was even born: Donnie Hathaway, Stevie Wonder, and Johnny Mathis. Once, when asked who her role model was, Aaliyah replied: "Barbra Streisand in *A Star is Born.* Acting, singing—she does it all."

Aaliyah said that her mature taste in music came from her parents. As a young girl, she would often borrow their records, singing along with the performers. "My parents come from the time of Fred Astaire and Sammy Davis Jr.," she said to *Jet* magazine. "Back then those people had to do it all. They had to sing, dance, and act. So that's how I was trained."

"She would always shine amongst everybody because of the quality of her voice," said Kathleen Samul, a former Gesu kindergarten teacher. "We were looking for someone who could be versatile and not only sing the pop songs of the day, but someone who could also sing Broadway."

She would get her chance to shine on national television when she landed on Star Search at 10 years old. Sure, Star Search is a cheesy show, but it is a show where, every so often, young performers with real talent emerge—Destiny's Child was once on the show as was Christina Aguilera. Then again, Britney Spears and Justin Timberlake of 'NSync also appeared on Star Search—but they lost.

And so did Aaliyah. She sang "My Funny Valentine," a ballad that has been covered by countless jazz, pop and R&B singers, including Sammy Davis Jr., Ella Fitzgerald, and Sarah Vaughan. (Aaliyah had also heard her own mother, Diane, singing the song.) For the contest, Aaliyah wore a white dress her grandmother had made for her. When the decision was announced, and Aaliyah found out that she was getting the heave-ho, she did what probably any 10-year-old would do: she cried. Probably some 22-year-olds would have cried too. But, despite her loss, she made an impression on the show's host.

"There's a thing that you see when somebody walks out on stage," McMahon told *Vibe* magazine. "I call it 'the fire.' They got that inner fire, which has nothing to do with the schooling, nothing to do with the teacher, nothing to do with the parents. There is a desire in that person to please the audience. You see enough of it to recognize it. And that's what I saw with Aaliyah."

Aaliyah's cousin, Jomo, said that Aaliyah had a singing talent that went beyond volume and hitting high notes. Said Jomo: "I think on the outside she just had a kind of charisma where you had people that could belt it out harder than she could, or that had vocals that seemed more dynamic on the surface, but Aaliyah had a kind of charm with her voice. It was a jazzy, sexy, smooth kind of thing and I think that's what people gravitated to. Her uniqueness. She really took the craft of making music seriously. There was never a doubt to me and my dad that she would be a huge success because she had the passion for it."

The Star Search defeat was a setback, but Aaliyah quickly recovered. Luckily her family connections came through. Aaliyah's uncle, Barry Hankerson, was then married to R&B star Gladys Knight.

Hankerson subsequently arranged to have his 11-year-old niece join his wife for a few performances.

Knight has been an R&B superstar since the '50s. Born in Atlanta in 1944, Knight, like Aaliyah, had been a child star, appearing several times on television before she was even ten years old. Her backing group, the Pips, were formed in 1952 to provide entertainment for guests at a birthday party thrown for Gladys' older brother, Merald. The group, Gladys Knight and the Pips, went on to tour with such stars as Sam Cooke and Jackie Wilson before Knight was even 13 years old, and generated a string of hit songs including "If I Were Your Woman," and "Midnight Train to Georgia." The group combined soulful vocals, tight harmonies, and understated choreography. It was elegantly controlled soul music, the kind that could grow old gracefully. It had the vigor of youth and the entertainment smarts typically associated with veteran performers.

Knight, who had a perspective on child stardom based on her own personal experience, had this to say about Aaliyah: "I remember the day Aaliyah was born . . . it was a great beautiful day. I was married to her uncle and she immediately became a special part of my life, and I became Auntie Gladys to that wonderful little girl. I watched her grow up, and, with the rest of the world, saw her achieve success with her very special and unique talents. From an early age, I knew she had enormous talents, and an intrinsic gift."

During one stretch, Gladys Knight was playing five nights at Bally's Las Vegas Casino and Aaliyah came out each night. "I was able to learn a lot from that," said Aaliyah. "I began to work the stage and get the audience into it. I also learned how to have fun out there. It is something that I will never forget." Las Vegas is an intimidating place for any youngster, even if that youngster isn't about to perform in front of thousands of people. There are spotlights and gamblers, showgirls and hustlers. But Aaliyah came through each time, smoothly professional even at her young age, joining Knight in renditions of "Believe in Yourself," and even going solo on a performance of "Home," the show-stopping number from the *The Wiz*.

Knight was impressed. "When she first performed with me in Las Vegas, she was still quite young, but she already had it—that spark the world would later see and fall in love with . . . she brought joy to my heart, and I felt blessed to encourage and support her professionally and personally."

Aaliyah, for her part, was confident that she could pull it all off. "I've never really had that much of a problem with it, getting respect," she said. "It's how you carry yourself. I've always been a very mature person and I've always known what I wanted, and I go after it no matter what."

Aaliyah was on her way. She was about to finally live out her dream—and she was also about to face the biggest public relations nightmare of her life.

3 | age ain't nothing but a number

She was so sweet, always. She was one of the most beautiful people on the inside as well as out.

—Beyoncé Knowles of Destiny's Child on Aaliyah to MTV News

R. Kelly's real first name is Robert. It's not a bad name, but it's not necessarily an exciting one either. His abbreviation of his first name gives him a sense of mystery and a bit of coolness, something that sets him apart from all the ordinary Robs and Bobs and Roberts of the world.

Not long after Barry Hankerson hooked his niece up with his then-wife Gladys Knight, he came through for Aaliyah again. He had formed a new record company, Blackground Records, and after signing a distribution deal with Jive Records, a larger label, he brought the company his very first signing: Aaliyah. Jive Records then brought the singer together with one of their brightest talents: R.Kelly.

R.Kelly once said to the *Chicago Daily Herald:* "My life is controversial." R.Kelly raised eyebrows for one reason: sex. R&B music introduced overt sexuality into mainstream American pop. There had always been sex in music, but it was almost always polite, sublimated, hidden in social niceties and soothing lyrics. In the '50s, Little Richard thrust sex into American pop in a big way: leering, gyrating, grinding, bringing all the libido-powered energy of teenage America to the surface. Years later, Prince would break other pop music conventions, making the sex harder, weirder, throwing in winks at God and nods at bisexuality.

R.Kelly followed in the footsteps of the sexy soulmen who had come before him: Little Richard and Marvin Gaye, Rick James and Prince. Like Prince, his songs melded sexuality and religiosity; unlike Prince, he stayed away from rock and psychedelia, and instead injected his brand of funky soul with a dose of hip-hop. Like Aaliyah, Kelly began performing young—before he was even out of junior high school he was belting out songs on stages on the south side of Chicago, where he grew up. One night he sang the Stevie Wonder classic "Ribbon in the Sky" and he knew he'd found his calling. "That night it was like Spiderman being bit," he would be quoted as saying in *The Orange County Register.* "I discovered the power you get from being onstage."

"When I looked at Robert," Lena McLin, Kelly's high school music teacher said to *YSB* magazine, "I saw another Stevie Wonder, and I proceeded to tell him that. I saw in him creativity, honesty, sincerity, dedication, and excitement, and those are the ingredients for a composer and entertainer."

"I want to say it's better than sex, but I don't know," Kelly said of the thrill of live performance to *The Chicago Daily Herald.* "It's just an awesome, awesome feeling to be onstage and people, I guess, loving you. It's like—I guess it is better than sex. Love is better than sex. What is wrong with me? Yes, so yes. It's better than sex. There, I said it."

Kelly's first album, *Born in the '90s*—which was released in 1991 under the name R.Kelly and Public Announcement—got him a foothold in the world of R&B with such minor Black radio hits as "She's Got That Vibe" and "Honey Love." But it was his next set, the 1993's follow-up *12 Play,* that brought him to the attention of the mainstream. That album sold more than 4 million copies and generated such salacious hits as "Your Body's Callin." The album was both a paean to the street (one song was titled "Back to the Hood of Things") and a celebration of sex itself (another track was the not-too-subtly titled "I Like the Crotch on You"). But whatever you thought of the lyrics, the music was there and the vocals were there. Kelly could sing and he could write. It was a hard-to-resist package: a guy with the edge of a gangsta rapper and the sometimes Stevie Wonder-ish ability to shape a tuneful song. Now and again, in his music, Kelly would reach for something deeper, just to prove that he could. One song on *12 Play,* "Sadie," is about the passing of his beloved mother. Of course, the song is offered up alongside such tracks as "Bump 'n' Grind" in which Kelly lustily declares: "There ain't nuthin' wrong with a little bump and grind." And you know what? He was right. *12 Play* showed it was cool to express affection for your mom and love for the ladies. For Kelly, being a good son and getting some good sex were not incompatible.

"If I've offended any woman out there, I would want to say, 'I'm sorry,'" Kelly said to *The News and Observer* of Raleigh, North Carolina. "I want them to realize that this is show business. Just think of it as an entertainment piece."

So perhaps that's why he seemed to be the perfect match for Aaliyah. Before Kelly, she had been the perfect kid: tight with her parents, popular with her teachers, best friends with her brother. Kelly didn't get her to rebel against all that as much as he showed her how her own image of herself was not in opposition with the new image he wanted to help create: an image of suggestion, sensuality, and sly grace, all in a teen-aged package. "What I sing about either I've experienced or I want to experience," Kelly once said. "I love being around women. I love fashion shows and things like that. I'm a mama's boy. A lot of my friends think I should be with every woman on the planet. All I need is one."

When Aaliyah was 14, she and R.Kelly went into the studio and came out with her album debut, *Age Ain't Nothing But a Number.* The album, released in 1994, was executive produced by Barry Hankerson, but the wizard behind the curtain was the producer, R.Kelly, who wrote every track except for a cover of the Isley Brothers' hit "At Your Best (You are Love)." R.Kelly also played all the instruments except for a few additional guitar and keyboard parts.

Aaliyah's first single, the coolly erotic, undulating "Back & Forth," went to number one on the R&B charts where it ironically, or perhaps appropriately, unseated R.Kelly's single, "Your Body's Callin." Pop icon Madonna, always on the lookout for whatever was hip and street, later sampled some of Aaliyah's "Back & Forth" for her single "Inside of Me" off of her 1994 album *Bedtime Stories.* "I know having him [R.Kelly] on the single helped it get attention," said Aaliyah to *The Baltimore Sun.* "Without him it would have been harder to get airplay. I'm just thankful for the break. If I had no talent and had nothing to offer, I'd probably feel funny if people were giving him all the credit. But I know I can sing and a lot of the success is because of me."

Kelly was the king of the charts and Aaliyah was his queen. Kelly and Aaliyah started appearing everywhere together, sometimes dressed in matching outfits. One of her first public performances to push her debut album was at a special showcase at an urban music conference that was headlined by Kelly. "It's always Aaliyah and R.Kelly, R.Kelly and Aaliyah," Aaliyah said in December of 1994. "I don't mind being called his protégé because that's what I am."

One of the biggest traps in music, and perhaps any artistic endeavor, is to fall under the sway of some other performer. Britney Spears is often written off—perhaps correctly—as a younger, less interesting version of Madonna. Lenny Kravitz—perhaps incorrectly—is often dismissed as a latter-day ripoff of Jimi Hendrix, Prince, or basically any African-American performer who ever blended rock with soul and played a guitar.

Comparisons are even tougher, however, for female artists. Women artists are often used as muses by their male counterparts—the women provide the inspiration and spark the creative fire, and the men get the credit. In fact, there are cases throughout history in which women were systematically shut out from high-profile forms of creative expression, or, at the very least, forced to radically alter their artistic approach to conform to prevailing mores. All three of the Brontë sisters believed, with a good deal of evidence to support their claims, that publishers would never accept the work of women, so Charlotte's *Jane Eyre,* Emily's *Wuthering Heights,* and Anne's *Agnes Grey* were all originally published under male pseudonyms: Currer, Ellis, and Acton Bell, respectively.

Over the years, the artistic abilities of women have been disparaged by some of the greatest male intellectuals and critics. "Girls begin to talk and to stand on their feet sooner than boys because weeds grow more quickly than good crops," Martin Luther said in 1533. "Instead of calling them beautiful, there would be more warrant for describing women as the unaesthetic sex. Neither for music, nor for poetry, nor for fine art, have they really and truly any sense or susceptibility," said the philosopher Arthur Schopenhauer in 1851. Critic William Gass declared that female writers "lack that blood-congested genital drive which energizes every great style." And critic Robert Graves held that "A woman who concerns herself with poetry" should either be a "silent muse" or "should be the muse in the complete sense . . . and should write with antique authority."

To women with the creative fire burning within them, being an object of some other artist's art, relegating one's self to inspiring another's act of creation, could provoke frustration, rage, and even a wild state of mind that society would all too often label madness. *TIME* magazine, in an article headlined "Work of a Wife," on April 14, 1934, condescendingly reviewed an exhibition of Zelda Fitzgerald's art, comparing her to her husband, F. Scott Fitzgerald (author of *The Great Gatsby*). "There was a time when Mrs. Francis Scott Key Fitzgerald was a more fabulous character than her novel-writing husband," the article read. "That was when she was Zelda Sayre, a Montgomery, Alabama girl. . . . When she married Scott Fitzgerald in 1920, shortly after he published *This Side of Paradise* she lapsed into the semiobscurity of a wife of a famed novelist." Zelda later suffered from mental illness. The sculptor Camille Claudel (the lover of sculptor Auguste Rodin) and would-be writer Vivienne Eliot (wife of the poet T.S. Eliot) both went through emotional breakdowns. More recently, the white rapper Eminem composed a number of songs fantasizing about the murder of his wife, Kim. Then, after she tried (and failed) to take her own life and subsequently filed for divorce, the rapper reconciled with her and promptly began writing songs about her aborted suicide attempt.

Of course, not every woman with artistic aspirations has been forced to channel her dreams through some man. In some cases men and women inspired and challenged each other, and, in the final estimation, the female artist was judged by history to be as great, if not greater, than her male partner as in the cases of Ted Hughes and Sylvia Plath, Diego Rivera and Frieda Kahlo, and rappers Wyclef Jean and Lauryn Hill.

But women, more often than not, get the critical shaft when they are linked with or compared to male artists. Musicians Yoko Ono and John Lennon shared a close working relationship, collaborating on political actions, art installments, and musical compositions. Ono often took the lead role with dealing with the outside world. "In a relationship I think women really have sort of the wisdom to cope with society since they created it," she was quoted as saying in David Sheff's book *All We Are Saying*. "Men never developed the inner wisdom; they didn't have time. So most men do rely on women's inner wisdom, whether they express that or not." Although already an established rock star as a member of the Beatles by the time he met Ono, Lennon nonetheless attributed much of his success to his wife: "It is a teacher-pupil relationship. That's what people don't understand. She's the teacher and I'm the pupil. I'm the famous one, the one who's supposed to know everything, but she's my teacher. She's taught me everything I fucking know. She was there when I was the nowhere man." Still, many critics and most fans saw Lennon as the true talent of the pair and dismissed Yoko as a mere hanger-on.

The same pattern would repeat itself years later with Kurt Cobain and his wife Courtney Love. Although Love was already a successful performer with her band Hole before she met and married Cobain, the leader of the punk trio Nirvana, afterward, she was seen as riding his coattails, as trying to use her husband to establish herself as alt-rock royalty. Perhaps she was. But regardless of her intentions, she was undeniably a passionate and powerful rock and roll performer and Hole's album *Live Through This,* released shortly after her husband's death in 1994, is one of the better alt-rock albums of the '90s.

At the beginning of the 21st century the role of the muse may have arrived at a crossroads. While boundaries and barriers still exist, there certainly seem to be greater opportunities for female artists to express themselves than say, back when Yoko was attacked for supposedly breaking up the Beatles. But progress is neither smooth nor inevitable; it lurches between advancement, regression, and stagnation. It is arguable whether today's female artists are more respected today, necessarily, than the women of '60s. Eminem presents one vision of the future: drawing on his wife's suffering, perhaps pushing her to the edge of mental breakdown and receiving accolades for his supposed daring. Lauryn Hill presents another possible tomorrow. As a member of the Fugees, she played a secondary role behind Wyclef Jean, who was also her lover. As a solo artist, she tapped into the passion of her relationship to create an album, *The Miseducation of Lauryn Hill,* which was a critical and commercial breakthrough, and which had more of a cultural impact than anything her male counterparts in her old band had managed to produce.

Aaliyah, in her relationship with Kelly, clearly lost a bit of her own personality. She really wasn't all that street, she really wasn't all that hard, but if she wanted to hang with her mentor, and if she wanted to successfully convey the edge of the hip-hop/soul hybrid music he had fashioned for her, it seemed as if she had to play the part of a baggy-clothes-wearing, dark-glasses-sporting, gangsta girl. Her image, from jump, was slightly mysterious—her eyes were often hidden behind dark glasses in her photo shoots. She tended to dress in black clothing or leather. And in almost all of her promotional shots, she is unsmiling, her chin set, her expression a bit dour. Was this the same Aaliyah that played an orphan in *Annie*? "What's the real me? It's hard to say," Aaliyah said. "I have a feeling for the hard-core street life, but I like to hang out in malls. I'm definitely going to college, and I'd like to get a doctorate in music history, with a minor in engineering. But I love singing more than anything. What does that say about me?"

Kelly, too, was engaged in an identity struggle. Good artists are often influenced by the trailblazing performers who have come before them. It takes a truly great artist, however, to break free and find one's own separate path. Kelly was on a Marvin Gaye trip, whether he consciously knew it or not. Gaye, back in the day, had met a younger woman while he was recording his album, *Let's Get it On.* The woman, Janis Hunter, was 16 years old at the time—17 years Gaye's junior. The two would later marry. When Kelly hooked up with Aaliyah, she was age 15 and Kelly was 27. Like Gaye, Kelly, according to some reports, married his young charge.

Or did he? In 1994, *Vibe* magazine published an article claiming that Aaliyah and Kelly had married and even published what *Vibe* claimed was the marriage certificate. "Our research editor found the marriage certificate by going through the public records office of Illinois where it is filed," Danyel Smith, who wrote the *Vibe* story, said later. "We wouldn't have printed it if we thought we could get sued. Our lawyers check everything. We stand by the story, we still believe the marriage took place."

Kelly and Aaliyah, however, both denied that the marriage occurred and even denied that their relationship had ever moved beyond friendship. "I saw [the *Vibe* article], but I don't really comment on that because I know it's not true," she said in December of 1994. "When people ask me, I tell them, 'Hey don't believe all that mess. We're close and people took it the wrong way.' "

"I've told people time and time again that I'm not married," Kelly said in November of 1995. "I'm truly not married. For the final time. I'm not married to Aaliyah whatever *Vibe* magazine wrote."

"I don't even wanna conversate on that," Kelly continued. "You get all kinds of things in the papers. Aaliyah is my best friend but we are not married and that's it. We're not gonna let the media get to us. We've talked about it. Her mum had talked to her about it too. We just laugh and move on. They don't know. They don't know what's really going on in my life."

There's something of a tradition in rock and roll of superstar musicians getting involved with young women. Jerry Lee Lewis and Elvis Presley both became intimate with and ultimately married teenage girls who were much younger than they were at the time. Rock stars and soulmen get a lot of action. If you ever spent time out on the road with a singer of even moderate popularity, you've seen how they are presented with a startling number of sexual opportunities from a stunningly wide range of beautiful women. But it's not as much fun as you might think.

In the end, the faces blur, the experiences melt away, and all you seem to be left with is a numbing emptiness. Teenaged women, in their innocence, in their immaculacy, must look awfully attractive to jaded pop stars who've lived too hard and seen too much.

But the tabloidy nature of the purported May–December relationship was too much for the two stars to take. Although Kelly's songs were dominating the charts and Aaliyah's album was riding high, at every interview, at every press stop, someone would ask them a question—or perhaps dozens of questions—about the rumored affair. Were they married? Were they not married? Questions about one's personal, intimate life are tough for adults to handle; they're tough for presidents of the United States to handle. For Aaliyah, they became frustrating, and she gradually realized the questions were turning her into a creature of the tabloids when she wanted to be a real star.

"It was a painful time for me and my family," she would tell a reporter in 1996, "but I got through it. That's why I'm proud to say I'm a strong person. I'm a survivor and I can handle anything. I'm very confident about that. I come from a very strong family and they are always there to protect me. If I need any help I'll just call on my mummy and daddy or my brother to whom I'm very close."

A break with Kelly became almost inevitable.

Even before the controversy broke, Aaliyah had set her sights on branching out beyond her mentor. "Of course there's a connection with me and Robert because he did write the whole album," said Aaliyah in December of 1994. "But as far as the second album goes, he will probably do some songs, but it won't be a whole project."

She also said: "R.Kelly is a wonderful producer and a wonderful artist. He's all good, but that time was very tense, so it's not really appropriate for us to see each other."

Aaliyah was young, but she knew what she wanted. She wanted to be a solo star—not part of a constellation. "I do see myself becoming my own artist," she said to *The Chicago Sun-Times.* "If you know your own style and you're sure of yourself, you can definitely overcome the whole protégé thing."

But could she really make it on her own?

4 | soul searching

She had a refreshing outlook for one so young, with true respect for her art and for her elders.

—Gladys Knight on Aaliyah

In the early '90s, alternative rock and gangsta rap were all the rage. Pearl Jam, Nirvana, the Smashing Pumpkins, and other alt-rock outfits were breaking new ground, setting sales records, and generally bringing new excitement to rock and roll. The groupie-chasing, party-giving, big-hair growing metal groups of the '80s had been pushed aside. The alt-rockers were seen as real, as relevant, as having something to say. After years of empty-calorie music, after a decade of George Michael's butt and Paula Abdul's cartoon dance moves, the public wanted something meaningful in their entertainment. To quote "Smells Like Teen Spirit," Kurt

Cobain's breakthrough anthem of teen angst, they were all saying, "Here we are now, entertain us."

Along with the alt-rockers, the gangsta rappers were there too, ready to do just that. The early '90s saw the rise of gangsta rap, of Dr. Dre and Snoop Doggy Dogg, of low-riding, *Boyz N The Hood*-quoting, thug-life-livin' rappers whose music professed to reflect what was really going down on the streets. So what if it was almost as much of a caricature of street life as the heavy metal acts had been an exaggeration of masculinity? Gangsta rap sounded truthful, it looked fresh, and it was taking over the charts.

Age Ain't Nothing But a Number introduced a breakthrough R&B sound to American music. It wasn't quite soul and it wasn't quite hip-hop. Of course, the queen of hip-hop soul, Mary J. Blige, had explored similar territory years before. But Blige, with her ghetto fabulous fashion sense, rough attitude, and drama-filled personal life was clearly a singer of the streets who, at that time, only gave a passing nod to more upscale sophistication. Although Aaliyah's debut album starts out advising listeners how to play her music in their Jeeps, her songs were also for all the beemers and Acuras out there as well. "My singing style is very soft, my signature is falsetto with a breathy tone," Aaliyah would say later. "The tracks come at you kind of tough, a bit edgy, hip-hop, but the vocals can be very soothing. I like that."

That was the winning formula of *Age Ain't Nothing But a Number:* soft vocals riding on hard beats. There was something for everyone in that mix. Alt rock and hip-hop fans looking for something harder could find elements they liked in the raw rhythms of Aaliyah's tracks. Pop music and R&B fans searching for something more soothing could find what they wanted in Aaliyah's tender vocals. While other R&B singers turned their songs into Sunday morning choir practice or Monday morning aerobics class, Aaliyah's singing style was relaxed, laid back, calm. She wasn't trying to overwhelm you with her passion, she wasn't trying to pound you down, Patti LaBelle-like, with her pipes. Aaliyah was trying to have a conversation. The contrast between her placid vocals and her harder, urban rhythms was intriguing; it caught the ear and drew the listener in.

When she came out in 1994, Aaliyah was virtually alone in her new sound. She didn't seem to quite fit anywhere. Was she R&B? Was she hip-hop? *What* was she? Radio programmers, record labels, and music critics love to squeeze artists into boxes. They love to create new terms to describe artists and sketch out new categories: death metal, Americana, drum 'n' bass, nortec. And musicians, generally, hate it. To be categorized is to be defined, and that implies limitations of some sort, places where your particular kind of music should and should not go.

And, of course, from an artist's perspective, art should have no limits. Products have labels so we can identify them by manufacturer and by price. Artists hate to be treated like products. "Lyrically I want things to be different," Aaliyah told *Blues & Soul* magazine. "Very deep. I love deep songs. I admire Stevie Wonder because he's someone that can take a love song and really put you in a whole 'nother place. I want to touch everybody. I think I'm a sweet person, very laid back but I'm also very complex . . . I want my music and the work that I do to stress that. From my perspective it can't be one dimensional. It must have depth."

Paul Hunter, a video director who helmed some of Aaliyah's best clips, said he would sometimes talk to her about where she fit in on the radio. Aaliyah's response to him was surprising. "She didn't like the typical thing," said Hunter. "She always told me when she'd turn on the radio she didn't want her songs to be easy to program. She didn't want to be lumped in with everybody else. She wanted her work to stand out."

Although Aaliyah might have rejected the label—like any true artist—her work really was part of an emerging genre in R&B and hip-hop. It could be called many things: alternative R&B, alternative soul, progressive soul, new soul or, perhaps the most popular name—neosoul.

Now, neosoul wasn't a new genre and it wasn't an

old one either. It was a musical form that had roots in the past but was constantly looking towards the future. Almost no neosoul artist would actually admit to being a neosoul artist, but they all had undeniable similarities that linked them together as a genre, as a movement, and as a musical force. And one of the most important things neosoul artists shared was this: They all wanted to be different.

The success of alt-rock and hip-hop in the mid-'90s had left R&B on the outs with critics. Though only-one-name-needed divas like Mariah and Whitney and Toni were at the top of the charts, soul music was generally seen by the media and the mostly rock-loving critical intelligentsia as weak, as disposable, as so not cool. Boyz II Men (who would later be shamelessly ripped off, style-wise, by Backstreet Boys) were moving units and filling performance venues, but they got little respect from music writers. Alt-rock and hip-hop were exploring life and how to live it: the alt-rockers were talking about tough subjects like alienation and suicide, teenage rebellion and social decay; rappers were talking about police brutality and smoking weed, street crime and racism. R&B singers, for the most part, were just talking about love, and to many rap and rock fans, it seemed as if they were doing so in obvious, overemotional ways.

Neosoul artists, however, were reclaiming some

of the creative fire from other genres of music. The social critic Frantz Fanon, in his landmark work of revolutionary theory, *The Wretched of the Earth,* stated that "the colonized man who writes for his people ought to use the past with the intention of opening the future." In fact, neosoul artists tended to be well versed in the past. They knew about Marvin Gaye. They had all studied the complete works of Stevie Wonder. They revered the soul-rock of Prince, the psychedelic soul of Sly and the Family Stone, and the vocal genius of Aretha Franklin. The neosoul singer D'Angelo recorded his album *Voodoo* at Electric Lady Studios, Jimi Hendrix's old studio. Neosoul diva Erykah Badu sings a passage from a Stevie Wonder song in the middle of one of her own numbers. And Angie Stone, another neosoul sister, performed a duet with Prince.

In fact, before there was a name for it, Prince had been carrying a torch for neosoul for decades, refusing to make R&B that played by the rules or fit into comfortable formats. In the mid-'90s, he was suddenly joined by a host of other soul artists who also wanted to break boundaries.

In 1995, neosoul singer D'Angelo released his breakthrough album *Brown Sugar.* On that CD, he gives a nod to the past, with his gliding cover of the Smokey Robinson song "Crusin'." But on his other material, he mints his own sound, with golden humming keyboards and sensual vocals and unhurried melodies. In an age of lowriders and gang banging anthems, D'Angelo helped make the image of the soulman cool again. His songs were polished without being slick and smart without being pretentious. He made music that clearly aspired to be art but wasn't afraid to get down and make people dance. His follow-up release, "Voodoo," was the best album released in the year 2000.

Erykah Badu, with her 1997 debut album *Baduizm,* brought an iconoclastic spirit to soul music, with her towering Afrocentric headwraps, incense candles, and quirky lyrics. Until Badu, most contemporary soul divas looked like supermodels and dressed like them too. Badu was beautiful and elegant, but she was fashionable on her own terms. Sometimes she wore dreads. One time she shaved her head bald. Her music was about all sorts of things: love, police brutality, and getting in touch with one's inner spirit. But mostly it was about being free to sound like whatever you wanted to sound like, and to sing about whatever you wanted to explore artistically.

Lauryn Hill came out with another landmark neosoul album in 1998 with *The Miseducation of Lauryn Hill.* Her album was both hip-hop and something more. She rapped and she sang, she wrote lyrics that were deeply personal (including one song, "Zion," about her decision not to abort her child) and songs about society at large. She paid homage to the past (the track "Forgive Them Father" samples the Bob Marley song "Concrete Jungle") while remaining completely and utterly modern. The album's opening cut is a jarring, passionate hip-hop song titled "Lost Ones." Hill's album was a breakthrough for neosoul and for hip-hop, and it won Album of the Year at the 1999 Grammy Awards. "Sometimes it's hard to really make any statements when you know the industry caters to hit singles rather than to developing artists," Hill once told me. "[But] I definitely felt like I wanted to push the envelope of hip-hop. It was very important to me that the music be very raw . . . and that there be a lot of live instrumentation."

Neosoul albums haven't always sold well. In fact, more than not, they have sold poorly. Bassist/rapper/neosoul singer Me'Shell NdegéOcello has released a number of superlative albums, from her 1993 debut CD *Plantation Lullabies* to 2001's *Cookie: The Anthropological Mix Tape.* She scored a mainstream hit when she performed a duet alongside John Mellencamp in 1994 (the song "Wild Night"), but, even after that success, her solo work continued to struggle for radio airplay and for sales. But, increasingly, neosoul albums are doing better and better on the charts. Lauryn Hill, Maxwell, D'Angelo, and Alicia Keys have all had number one albums. At first, it seems, neosoul acts may have been written off as watered down versions of blackness. But by the beginning of the 21st century, there was a growing awareness that neosoul artists were actually more daring, and more inclusive, than hardcore gangsta rappers in their vision of African-American culture. Neosoul artists weren't creating caricatures and stereotypes to scare and provoke the public; they were offering up something more nuanced.

The poet Langston Hughes, in a speech he gave in 1966 entitled "Black Writers in a Troubled World," once addressed some of the issues faced by artists of color in the United States. "The [Black] writer in the United States has always had—has always been forced to have in spite of himself, two audiences, one black, one white. And, as long has been America's dilemma, seldom 'the twain shall meet.' The fence between the two audiences is the color bar which in reality stretches around the world. Writers who feel they must straddle this fence, perforce acquire a split personality. Writers who do not care whether they straddle the fence of color or not, are usually the best writers, attempting at least to let their art leap the barriers of color, poverty, or whatever other roadblocks to artistic truth there may be. Unfortunately, some writers get artistic truth and financial success mixed up, get critical acclaim and personal integrity confused. Such are the dilemmas which the double audience creates. Which set of readers to please—the white, the black or both readers at once?"

Aaliyah was on the cutting edge of this movement that didn't want to be a movement. She was part of this group of performers that steadfastedly resisted being grouped with anyone else. She, along with other neosoul stars, refused to be bound in by fences and barriers, color lines and restrictions. They were free, in part, because they accepted that their music was on the fringes of pop and because they didn't court mass acceptance—if it came, fine, and many neosoul stars believed that, eventually, it would come. And by the close of the '90s, it did. The reason neosoul grew in influence was due to an emerging group of music fans who wanted to hear music that reflected more of the African-American experience. Gangsta rap showed a part of it, but only a small part, and sometimes a distorted part. Not all black people, of course, were rolling like Snoop Dogg. Not all black people were holding it down like Dr. Dre.

When I wrote an article for *TIME* about the rise of neosoul in 1998, D'Angelo had this to say: "I avoid the radio. I want to take hip-hop and funk and make it new again. I want to take it back to basics. I'm tired of all the synthetic stuff."

He continued: "The mid-to-late '60s was the golden age of soul and funk. It wasn't like now, where you have one producer working for a slew of artists, who all sound the same. Artists are no longer self-contained and are more prone to conform. In the '60s, people were defying what people expected. That's what's missing now."

Maxwell, who I talked to for that *TIME* story, also argued that Black music needed shaking up. Neosoul artists seemed to believe that Black music should be all music—it should incorporate jazz and rock and hip-hop and gospel and reggae and electronica and whatever else worked or felt right. The primary pop musical forms in America—soul, rap, rock, blues, and country—were all rooted in African American culture, so it made no sense for African American artists to cut themselves off from these influences. Erykah Badu has dueted with reggae star Stephen Marley (son of Bob Marley); Lauryn Hill, on her debut album brought in Latin rocker Carlos Santana to provide a guitar solo; Maxwell has performed songs in Spanish and covered songs by British art-rocker Kate Bush.

"I think people are a lot smarter than they are credited with being," said Maxwell. "I like to challenge what some people think most people will accept and listen to, particularly African Americans and particularly in the R&B genre. To me, it's important to reflect the alternative."

Aaliyah, as a teenager, was already a trailblazer; she was on the scene before the wave of neosoul acts really hit. Her genre-busting attitude and sound would help clear the way for artists such as Jill Scott, Alicia Keys, Bilal, and others in the late '90s and the early '00s. "They were calling me the prototype for the girl of the '90s," Aaliyah told *Echoes* magazine in August 2001. "To be called a trendsetter was wonderful."

Still, Aaliyah was conscious of copycats. She didn't mind people following in her footsteps, she just didn't want them stepping on her toes. "You go through a stage in your life when you try and discover who you are and once you do that's a wonderful thing. When someone kinda bites that, that's kind of annoying. It's the highest form of compliment when someone copies what you do. But it can get to the point where it can get taken too far, and that's totally aggravating. That's when I don't like it."

But, after her debut CD, Aaliyah still felt as if she had a ways to go. *Age Ain't Nothing But a Number* was a fine album, but she knew, in her heart, that it wasn't entirely her album. And that, as long as she was with a brand-name, big-shot producer like R.Kelly, she would never be seen as a separate, true artist. "I kinda sat back on the first album and observed a lot of what was going on," Aaliyah said. She was willing to wait then, but she was quickly growing up.

And she was on the lookout. She took a break for

a few years and focused on her schoolwork. All the while though she was dreaming of finding another producer, one that would help to bring out the sounds that were in her head and in her heart. "It's fun to be creative and innovative and come up with something crazy," Aaliyah told the *Calgary Herald*. "So I needed people to work with who are not going to be afraid to take it to the left a bit."

She would soon take that sharp left turn.

5 | one in a million

> The reason she was a star to everybody is that she had her own identity. Nobody else sounded like Aaliyah.
>
> —Jermaine Dupri

Timbaland, one of the most respected music producers of his generation, can't read or write music using traditional notation. Then again Paul McCartney, who, along with John Lennon, was the chief songwriter for the Beatles, also lacked the ability to read or write music. Of course musicians can always gain by mastering their craft, learning how to play multiple instruments, going to school or even engaging in some sort of independent study so that they can put pen to paper and write out their compositions. But perhaps there's something to be said for finding one's own way in the music industry, bypassing the traditional structures and ways of doing things. Perhaps, by doing that, some artists are able to hear things that other performers never even think to listen for.

Timbaland's real name is Timothy Mosley. Hip-hop, even more so than rock, is a world ruled by producers. Dr. Dre helped make Snoop Doggy Dogg and, as an encore, he helped create naughty-boy white rapper Eminem as well. Sean "P. Diddy" Combs isn't much of a rapper and he isn't much of a dancer, but by making his name as a producer he's managed to get the public to not only take him seriously in those fields, he's even branched out to become a fashion designer. Producers are important in hip-hop because gaining entrée into the rap world isn't just about music, it's about words. If you can rhyme, if you've got verbal dexterity, if you can string together a series of clever phrases and jokes and putdowns, you're in. Once you're in, however, you're gonna need some music.

And that's Timbaland's specialty. "I started with an old DJ set scratching," Timbaland, who grew up in Norfolk, Virginia, told *The Record* of Bergen County, New Jersey. "I always wanted to be a DJ instead of a producer." Once he set upon his chosen field, however, he aimed for the top. "I told people . . . I was going to change radio, and that's what I did," he said. Timbaland's beats didn't sound like everybody else's. Other producers reveled in the predictability of machine-generated rhythms; they made them harder and faster and more in your face. Timbaland made beats that were elusive, unpredictable. They were synthetic, but they had a kind of artificial intelligence and his rhythms had a kind of organized randomness. The beats he would lay down would stutter, stop, start again: daring you to follow them. Other producers' beats lulled you to sleep or hammered you into submission. Timbaland's rhythms kept you awake, leaving you eager to find out just where they'd go next.

So it was a smart move when Aaliyah hooked up with Timbaland for her 1996 sophomore album *One in a Million.* At that time, producers weren't as visible in R&B as they were in hip-hop, but their influence was still strong. Most soul divas turned their albums into carnivals of production, with each track produced (and often overproduced) by some hit-making studio wizard with a big rep in the industry and a recognizable sound on the radio. Guys like David Foster, a producer known for big sappy mainstream production jobs that went straight to number one. Or Babyface, a producer known for wet-nosed, tail-wagging puppy dog-friendly soul-pop songs that the radio couldn't get enough of. Divas—like Whitney Houston, like Mariah Carey, like Celine Dion—were expected to put themselves into the hands of such producers and then just wait for the gold and platinum records to roll in. Aaliyah, after working with, and making a break from, R.Kelly, was widely expected to follow suit.

In many ways, the music industry is based on the pursuit of mediocrity. The mediocre is desired by music industry suits largely because bad artists are easier to control than great ones. Great ones call the shots, take wild chances and are irreplaceable. Crummy artists owe their lives and careers to whoever it is that gave them their record deal. Because of that, they'll sign autographs until their hands bleed, they'll make as many personal appearances as you want, they'll work with whatever producers you assign to them and, if they do happen to get out of hand, there are a thousand more mediocrities waiting to replace them.

Most music industry suits, despite what's written in the papers, spilled across the pages of glossy magazines, and blared from video screens, aren't really interested in The Next Big Thing. What they're really on the lookout for is the Last Big Thing. They want a clone of whatever is hot right now. Finding another Bob Marley or Bob Dylan or Lauryn Hill is a shot in the dark; finding five boy band clowns who can sing just like the last five boy band clowns is easy and, in the short term, sometimes profitable.

So that's where the usual suspects come in, the usual producers. Studio guys like David Foster make everyone sound like everyone else, increasing the likelihood that whatever pop clone the record industry suits are pushing will at least get heard on the radio. And that was exactly what Aaliyah, at the tender age of 17, decided she didn't want to play into. Sure, she trusted producers with her sound, but she didn't let her producers play her. Instead, she played them. In fact, the instrument that Aaliyah played best was other people. She didn't do this in a bad way, she did it in a way that was beneficial for all concerned. She knew how to gather a good team around her, team that could translate her personal aesthetic into music that wouldn't get lost in a crowd but would make her stand out.

So Aaliyah hooked up with Timbaland, and, in doing so, created a new career blueprint for other singers to follow. "I trust Tim totally," said Aaliyah to *ID* magazine. "When he has a crazy track that he doesn't think anyone else will do, he knows that I'll try it." Timbaland, then 24 years old, was known, but unproven; respected, but mostly untested. Aaliyah and her creative team decided that getting somebody who was young, hungry and good was preferable to landing a producer who was proven but predictable. Aaliyah also wanted to broaden her own horizons. "As I work with new people," Aaliyah would say later, "I like to pick up all these different sounds."

Over the years, Aaliyah and Timbaland developed

a professional bond that deepened into mutual respect and admiration. "There's a friendship there as well," Aaliyah said in later years. "When we work together, it is always fun . . . When we go into a studio it's like going into a club. It's like friends hanging out and kicking it. We laugh, we joke and then we work. The chemistry is just beyond words.

"Tim has to be comfortable with you to let his guard down," Aaliyah told *Mixmag.* "He'll tell a couple of jokes, be a little silly—when we work together we have fun. He doesn't do that with everyone, he's reserved and laid-back. He knows me better than anyone else."

Her next smart move was asking Missy "Misdemeanor" Elliott to work on *One in a Million.* Said Aaliyah: "When we met, there was a bond that was established real quickly. A friendship formed and we built our studio relationship from that." Elliott, like Timbaland, was, at the time, young and mostly untested. But she had a fresh approach to making hip-hop soul tracks. She wasn't afraid to be goofy, her rhythms were unexpected and loose-limbed. She was the clown princess of hip-hop-soul. "Missy's hilarious," Aaliyah said. "She very sweet and she's funny all the time and I love to laugh. Even if she's a little sad she finds something to giggle about. So we have a ball together."

Missy Elliott told me in October of 2001 that with

One in a Million, Aaliyah gave her and her producing/songwriting partner Timbaland their first big break. "Of course we was nobody and we didn't have no records out or nothing," Elliott said to me. "Ain't nobody know what a Missy Elliott was or a Timbaland. People only knew me from guest appearing on records, not for writing."

So in early 1996, Elliott and Timbaland flew off to record with Aaliyah. "When I first met Aaliyah it was in Detroit," said Elliott. "Now, to me, Detroit is really country. Not country country, as in southern country. Just the studio there had different kind of mixing boards than we were used to working on, and when we got there we was joking, 'Man how can you record out of here? Because this is like some old Motown equipment!' So it was funny just to even go to Detroit because we had never been to that city before."

Although the recording facilities weren't quite what they imagined, Timbaland and Elliott, still up-and-comers at the time, were excited about working with a hot artist. Said Elliott: "Aaliyah put us up in a great hotel. It was like really major. It had a living room and a bedroom. We felt like 'Man we're hanging with a superstar.' Of course we were a little bit nervous because this was someone who was already established, already a double-platinum artist. And when we got there she made us feel like she knew us all her life. She wasn't like 'I'm Aaliyah and I've had this hit record and that hit record.' She made us feel like we had already had a million hit records together."

I talked to Timbaland a few weeks after Aaliyah's passing and, although he was heartbroken, he still remembered all the good times. "Working with Aaliyah in the studio," Timbaland told me, "was like being in a funhouse." He said that Aaliyah was always open to new ideas, always willing to approach things from an unusual angle. "She liked to go to the far left like I did," he told me. Aaliyah was also willing to put in a lot of effort. Her recording sessions with Timbaland would typically last for eight hours at a time; sometimes, if things were going well, they would last all night. It was work, but it was also something more. Says Timbaland: "I still look at her as my little sister." Timbaland said one thing that really stood out about Aaliyah was her voice. "That hummingbird sound that she always brought," he said. "It was soft, real soft." Combined with his beats, he said, "It changed radio. Everything changed."

One in a Million, released in 1996, kicks off with Aaliyah declaring, in a confident coo, that "I got the beats for the streets." But, in reality, it was an album for anyone who cared about innovative music. The album's cover art continued to build Aaliyah's image of mysterious sexuality: It featured a picture of the singer wearing impenetrably black dark glasses, her expression hard to read, her eyes impossible to see. Again, she is unsmiling.

The music was similarly restrained. The title track, produced by both Timbaland and Elliott, is a quiet masterpiece of insinuation; it never explodes, it never gets loud, it keeps all its passion burbling beneath the surface. Another track, "If Your Girl Only Knew," also produced by Timbaland and Elliott, has a threatening funkiness that shades the song without making it bitter or overly hard.

"Of course, coming behind R.Kelly you've got to come correct," said Elliott. "He's the balladeer of balladeers, he's the hip-hop writer of hip-hop writers. Plus, he had established a sound for Aaliyah already. But I felt like if she was venturing to do something on her own, why give her what R.Kelly already gave her? Because then she might as well have asked R.Kelly to do the album.

"So I think we just did what we do anyways. That's what made it work. We wasn't trying to be R.Kelly. It was just do what we do and see how it comes out. There was pressure there but we ended up saying 'Ain't no need to compete against him, we're just gonna be us.' "

Elliott and Timbaland, however, did adjust their styles to suit their new young star. Said Elliott: "Of course Aaliyah was still young when we first began to work with her, so we had to be very careful about lyrical content. But I think we just wanted to make a futuristic sound for her. And there couldn't have been anybody else better to do it because we probably wouldn't have been able to come right out with a sound like that because we weren't known. Because Aaliyah was already known and had already had hits, it was easier for people to accept her coming out with something far left."

One of the most impressive things about the album is Aaliyah's willingness to let the beats be the star. Many singers push to have their vocals elevated above the mix, to make sure their singing is heard above all else. Aaliyah often let her vocals get carried away with the beat, letting her voice and the listener get swept away by the rhythms of the song. "I think what made Aaliyah stand out was the pureness and softness of her voice," said Elliott. "It was soft but still powerful in its own way, without having to scream. There was a subtlety about it."

One in a Million also gave Aaliyah a chance to celebrate the music of one of her childhood heroes: Marvin Gaye. On one track she serves up a hip-hop-infused remake of Gaye's dance classic "Got to Give It Up." The song allowed Aaliyah to bridge generations. Older listeners got to relive some of the great music of their youth while younger listeners were introduced to a whole new world of soul. In the video for the song, Aaliyah even performs alongside a ghostly, dancing image of Gaye.

One in a Million sold quite well but it accomplished something even more important. It established Aaliyah as a career artist and proved that she was capable of artistry without the input of R.Kelly. The music industry is rarely kind to female protégées. In the '80s, Prince introduced the world to Vanity 6, Apollonia, and numerous other sexy female acts, none of whom was able to succeed in the long term.

One reason for Aaliyah's success beyond her teenage years is the fact that she continued to mature. Many child stars—Debbie Gibson, Tiffany, the majority of the members of New Kids on the Block—freeze-dry in our memory as eternal children. Even as they grow older, even as their voices change, their features shift and their bodies sag, we still look at them and see the youthful images that existed when we were first introduced to them. We project this image onto them and it warps, like a movie displayed on a warped screen. But in our eyes, they can never grow up. Part of this is because they have given us no other reason to be interested in them other than their precociousness, and so we continue to search for it, even when the star in question becomes old enough to collect on their 401 (k).

Aaliyah took steps to transcend precociousness. Even as her star rose, she continued to attend the Detroit High School for Fine and Performing Arts. The school, located in a rather weatherworn building on Rosa Parks Boulevard, is a haven for early developers and child entertainers with adult potential. Founded in 1992, it's a competitive, rigorous school whose atmosphere, can at times remind visitors of the movie *Fame*, a fictional musical about New York City's similar High School for the Performing Arts. At any point at DSA, as the Detroit school is called, you may see groups of kids singing harmony in the hallway or a young dancer practicing her steps. Classes here start early and run late. DSA is not easy to get into: Would-be students have to apply and then they have to audition just as they might, say, for a part in a Broadway production. The mayor of Detroit, Dennis Archer, once referred to DSA as "a crowning jewel of our city." When it was founded in 1992, there were only 90 students; now the high school has more than 500 enrolled. It's a mostly black school, but there is some diversity: The student body is 98 percent black and 2 percent white. The school's disciplines include dance, theater, visual arts, and music. Only students with a 2.5 GPA and above need apply. If, while at DSA, their grades fall below that level, they are asked to leave. 100 percent of the 2001 graduating class received acceptance to college—an amazing success rate by any standard.

Aaliyah, who majored not in music but in dance, graduated from DSA in 1997 with a 4.0 GPA. "I think sometimes people negate the fact that training is important," said Aaliyah. "I mean, I feel blessed to have that theory . . . all that helps you in the long run." Still, Aaliyah wasn't just about homework. While in high school, she still found time to star in an advertising campaign for Tommy Hilfiger jeans with Kidada Jones (Quincy Jones' daughter). Aaliyah was going multimedia.

Denise Davis-Cotton, the founder and principal of DSA, says Aaliyah was a standout student from the start. Davis-Cotton was at Aaliyah's entrance audition. Aaliyah, at that time, was 13 years old and getting ready to graduate from the 8th grade. Davis-Cotton had run into her parents at a movie theater and told them that her new school would be a great place for their budding young talent. So Aaliyah came in to audition. Davis-Cotton says that at the session Aaliyah sang a rendition of the hymn "Ave Maria"—all in Latin.

"She had a very clear voice, very distinct," says Davis-Cotton. "And she had a very expressive personality. She was also very cordial. That's what I remember from that audition." Aaliyah was accepted immediately.

While it was obvious that Aaliyah had exceptional talent, she was also good at blending in. She was a popular student and had lots of friends. She also tried, when she could, to share her musical success with others. She once invited her fellow classmates to come to the taping of one of her videos so they could participate in the experience. In addition, a couple of students signed on as backup dancers for Aaliyah while she attended DSA.

Entertainers often don't plan for the long runs, they live their lives gig to gig, paycheck to paycheck, hand to mouth. The ride, while you're on it, seems as if it will last forever; it seems there will always be crowds at the concerts, autograph seekers after the show, and media waiting back at the hotel or the apartment for a snapshot, starving for a stray quote. Aaliyah, from a young age, had old age in mind. She had seen the careers of performers such as Barbara Streisand and knew she wanted to follow a similar path.

Streisand was a singer, an actress, and a director; someone who seemed as if she could create popular, award-winning work in whatever field she chose. Aaliyah was ambitious, but not overly or unwisely so. If you ask most vocalists if they have an interest in writing songs, the majority will let hubris get the best of them and answer yes. Aaliyah, however, played to her strengths; she wanted to do it all, but only wanted to focus on the things she knew she could do well. She co-wrote one song with her brother and that was it. She decided writing wasn't her thing and that it was something she would delegate to others. But when she found she had a knack for dancing and acting, she latched onto those fields and continued to develop her abilities in them throughout her life.

Great artists often surprise us. There are some artists—the not so great ones—that have only one trick in them and they perform that trick, under differing guises and in differing ways, throughout their careers. Celine Dion, for example, has essentially been making the same album over and over, year after year. Great artists, the rare ones, have several acts within them. Bob Dylan is a folk/blues artist who famously electrified his sound in the '60s, combining cerebral lyricism with hard-hitting rock. Prince has gone through a number of career changes, from being an erotic provocateur to a psychedelic love child to ditching his name for an unpronounceable symbol to reclaiming his old name again and rediscovering his muse. Madonna, of course, changes her musical style and look from album to album, and, if you've ever seen her in concert, sometimes she does it from song to song.

Aaliyah's stylistic shifts, crammed into just a few

short years, were not as drastic but they did suggest that she was an artist who was on the move, who was never completely satisfied with what she had done in the past and who was constantly looking towards the future. You can hear her inventiveness in her music. Aaliyah also created a video image that helped capture her mystery.

6 | siren of the small screen

Every time I saw Aaliyah she was smarter and more focused.

—PAUL HUNTER, AWARD-WINNING MUSIC VIDEO DIRECTOR

It was a small moment. But it was the moment when Paul Hunter realized Aaliyah was cool.

Oh, he liked her when he first met her back in 1996. He had met her through her uncle, the head of Blackground, who had arranged a meeting between the two in a New York studio. She seemed smart and shy and fun, and so Hunter agreed to work with her at some point.

That point came when they shot a video for one of her songs, "One in a Million," in Los Angeles in 1996. Everything was going well, the project was on schedule, and it was time to move to another location. So the crew packed up and stuffed themselves into a car—and Aaliyah stuffed herself right in there with them. "I thought she was really cool," said Hunter. "She was like this young superstar and we need to go to the next location and she just rides over with the crew. She didn't call for a limo or anything. It was really cute. She was just a regular girl in that respect, y'know?"

Before Aaliyah broke into films she was breaking the mold in music videos. In the mid-'90s, around the time that she was making her "One in a Million" video, it seemed as if the video form was dead. Finished. Stick a fork in it. The form seemed to lack the power to surprise or even to entertain. Musicians were making videos because they had to, because MTV was the new radio, because perhaps they had a couple of hours to kill after a gig on Saturday. Increasingly, at that time, videos were a thing to ridicule and even MTV itself was in on the mocking. MTV's since-canceled series Beavis and Butt-head made fun of videos; VH-1's Pop-Up Videos seemed to say, with its very format, that videos weren't interesting enough to watch anymore unless there was supplementary information to keep you from turning the channel to the Food Network.

One move that helped save videos: name-checks. In the early '90s, MTV started putting director's names on the video credits; that meant filmmakers would get the credit—or blame—for what they did.

If you made a heavy metal video full of half-naked supermodels, your mom was gonna call you. If you made a brilliant video with references to German Expressionism and *The Seventh Seal,* perhaps Hollywood was going to call you. So the word began to spread. Videos could lead to feature films. And, not too mysteriously, the quality of videos began to go up.

Around this time a new wave of video wizards appeared on the scene: there was Hype Williams, who directed videos by Missy Elliott ("The Rain [Supa Dupa Fly]") and Mary J. Blige ("Everything"). There was the elegantly creepy work of Floria Sigismondi who directed videos for shock rocker Marilyn Manson (one featured him shaving his own armpit) and trip-hopper Tricky. And there was also prankster auteur Spike Jonze, the man behind Icelandic chanteuse Björk's "It's Oh So Quiet" (a video that explodes into a technicolor musical), the Beastie Boys' "Sabotage" (a take-off on '70s TV cop shows), and Weezer's "Buddy Holly" (a good-natured "Happy Days" sendup). Jonze also showed that videos could indeed lead to the big screen: After helming some MTV clips, he went on to direct the Oscar-nominated film *Being John Malkovich.*

Paul Hunter was one of the brightest video talents to come out of that wave. Hunter, who grew up in Queens, originally wanted to be a painter. "That's what probably stimulated my interest in color now," he said when I wrote a story about him in *TIME* in 1997. "I wanted to be Basquiat or Keith Haring." He embarked on a career as a still photographer but decided to study film at California State University at Northridge after visiting a movie set when his brother, an aspiring actor, got a part in an indie film. Hunter later dropped out: "I learned that I had to go out and hustle if I was going to make it, [that] I was going to have to go out and make films by whatever means I could."

Hunter's music videos have a lush look and a strong sense of style. His video of Puff Daddy's "All About the Benjamins" makes the song come alive with its rushing, forceful images. Hunter's directorial approach, mixing style and substance, was an excellent match for Aaliyah. From Day One, says Hunter, Aaliyah wanted her videos to stand out from clips by other R&B singers. "You can watch programming all day and see a certain type of video by female artists," says Hunter. "Then when one of hers comes on it's something special, something different to look at. That's what she was about."

Aaliyah's videos, for the most part, are about mood, not about storylines. They are usually lushly shot and infused with sexual tension, though not in overt and obvious ways. There are small shocks in her videos, but not graphic ones; she usually dances in her clips, but the sequences never look heavily choreographed. In general, Aaliyah's videos tend to have a languid, liquid feel. They flow past the eye—rivers of color and skin and light. While most videos on MTV tend to leave the viewer amped up and hyped up and full of energy, Aaliyah's videos feel like slow, firm back massages. While watching them the tension just seems to drain out of your body, leaving you with gentle melodies and insistent rhythms.

Aaliyah made a number of videos throughout her career, but a few stand out. In particular, two clips she made with Hunter, "One in a Million" (1996) and "We Need a Resolution" (2001) are particularly representative of her best video work. And because they almost bracket her career, they also show the ways in which she eventually grew as a video artist.

The video for "One in a Million" helped establish Aaliyah's signature style. It begins with her lying on a car hood, her midriff bare; it is a scene that is casually provocative. Aaliyah changes outfits through the short clip; she wears large dark glasses one moment, she wears a gold monocle-like eyepiece the next. She wears a leather top and leather pants, then we see her in a gold mesh top, and then we see her in a white tank top, her face bare, her hair swept over her left eye. The sets are futuristic in a ruined future, *Blade Runner* sort of way: In one sequence, it looks as if Aaliyah is inside a giant clock of some sort. Near the end of the clip, we see Aaliyah on the back of a motorcycle, heading someplace with someone. Nothing is explained, many things are suggested. Throughout the video the tone is both urban and urbane; it's a balance that Aaliyah would strike often throughout her career.

"She's just very comfortable in front of the camera," says Hunter. "When the camera is on she just lights up. She loves performing, she lives for this kind of work. She's like a big kid. It seemed like she was gonna be like that forever. Her spirit was so bright."

Hunter and Aaliyah had a concept for the video for "We Need a Resolution," the first song off Aaliyah's last album, *Aaliyah.* The idea was this: Aaliyah would play a character that was a sort of twisted version of herself. In the video, she was to be a reclusive, privileged celebrity, the kind that you only get to meet if you're another privileged celebrity. Hunter and Aaliyah wanted to capture the sense of a closed, kinky world, a place of leather and mystery, an abode of hidden entrances and secret rooms. Says Hunter: "She just wanted something simple, maybe just four setups. We wanted each of them to have a kind of beauty."

"So we talked about the idea behind it being that this woman is leading this really alternate lifestyle," says Hunter. "She's the ultimate celebrity. You'd never be able to drive down the street and see her, you'd never be able to just run into her in the grocery store. In the video you're just getting a sneak peek into her life and into her world."

"We Need a Resolution" begins with a crisp, cool shot of Aaliyah sitting down, giving the camera a confident, sultry look. She is wearing black, in front of a black background, and her black hair is blowing slightly in a breeze. Then the scenes begin to come at us faster. We see Aaliyah travelling in some sort of futuristic subway tube. We see close-ups of her face: her eyeshadow is dark, her lips are blood red. We see scenes from what we presume is her lair: in one sequence, we see Aaliyah in something like a meditation chamber, headphones on, levitating above the floor in a prone position. The scenes keep coming. There are images of eels, a relaxed dance sequence, and a scene in which a number of huge snakes slither around Aaliyah's body.

Interestingly, the snake scene was one of Aaliyah's favorites. "I handle one really big python, and it's really cool and very sexy," she told *USA Today.* "Snakes are very beautiful creatures to me. They're very mysterious and dangerous at the same time and I like that mix. I couldn't wait to shoot that scene."

Aaliyah, through her work in video, was also becoming more comfortable displaying her sexier side in public. "I've always had a sexy side," she told *Echoes* magazine. "I'm 22 years old and a young adult and that definitely will shine through in everything from the songs to the videos to how the songs will be when I tour."

However, she did have her limits. She wanted to be sexy and classy, and never wanted to sacrifice the latter to achieve the former. "It's hard to say what I'm gonna do tomorrow, let alone in a few years time," Aaliyah said. "I'm very conscious of my image, so everything I do I talk about with my manager. I'm not gonna go too far but I'm gonna be me and I'll embrace my sexiness for sure."

"We Need a Resolution" is one of Aaliyah's strangest videos and one of the weirder videos made by an R&B singer in recent years. It stands out because it doesn't explain; it intrigues because it doesn't offer standard come-on's, and it's beautiful to look at because it's not afraid to be a bit dirty. In one scene, Aaliyah is inexplicably smeared with mud. It's clearly the work of an artist who is comfortable with her image and confident that she can look good and appear desirable no matter what's she wearing. It was another step forward not just for Aaliyah, but for young female artists in general. Videos tended to put young female performers in a beauty cage. Their job was to look good at all times, to be perfect in all scenes. Aaliyah's smeared mud look was a rejection of that. It said to the viewer take me as I am. And I may well be dirty.

Aaliyah was a true video artist in that she was very

involved in the clips she appeared in and was very interested in making sure the visual message meshed well with the musical one. The two didn't have to match, they just needed to fit in some sort of subconscious way. There doesn't seem to be any connection between the lyrics of "One in a Million" and "We Need a Resolution" and the clips that accompanied them.

Aaliyah's style was on the cutting-edge of a hip-hop takeover of fashion that started in the '70s, gained momentum in the '80s, and came of age in the '90s. In 1999 I attended a party that Lauryn Hill hosted at an Emporio Armani store in downtown New York City. It was partly a charity event—the get-together was meant to help raise money for Hill's Refugee Project. But Armani also helped sponsor Hill's 28-city world tour. So there was Lauryn Hill, wandering through the aisles of the Armani store, meeting and greeting guests. "Lauryn is a really inspirational figure to me, a beautiful young woman with talent, heart, intelligence, and style," Armani said in 1999. "She is strong, very dedicated, and confident about what she can do in the world. She embodies precisely the values that I try to express with Emporio Armani." If that sounds like a press release, that's because it was. Hip-hop, by the end of the '90s, was part of the high fashion hype machine. But the most amazing part was that, in many cases, and certainly in the case of Hill, such associations with the kings and queens of haute couture cost the artists zero in terms of street credibility.

Jazz, pop, and rock have long had a major influence on style both in Europe and in America. In the '50s, the great jazz trumpeter Miles Davis appeared on the cover of his album *Kind of Blue* in a serene blue suit, forever associating his brand of cool jazz with an elegant form of dress. In the '60s, so called "Mods"—British kids with a love of modern jazz—began to popularize their very distinctive form of dress, which included neat tailored clothes, and their immaculate grooming. The Small Faces, The Who, and the Beatles helped bring variations of the Mod look out to the world. In the '60s, a wide range of women's clothing was churned out emblazoned with portraits of the Beatles—including stockings. In later decades, disheveled punk groups such as the Sex Pistols and gender-bending glam acts such as David Bowie also made their mark on the fashion world. In 1977, designer Zhandra Rhodes created a collection called "Conceptual Chic" that included ripped rayon jersey dresses ornamented with safety pins, ball-link chains and other punk-like objects.

But the arrival of hip-hop was a turning point for fashion. Musicians had been stylish in the past but they had usually held such associations at arm's length. It wasn't cool to be too conscious of one's clothes. It wasn't "rock and roll" to be associated too closely with any designer. This state of affairs often allowed other folks to make money off the looks that rockers had created. In the early '90s, fashion boutiques began to market the grunge look—knit caps and flannel shirts and long short pants—as alternative rockers looked on with horror and didn't make a dime.

Hip-hoppers had a different approach which not only changed the look of music, it also changed the fashion industry forever. Hip-hoppers willingly aligned themselves with designers and brands. Run-DMC signed a deal with Adidas shoes after rapping about them on their songs (like "My Adidas"). Other rappers started their own companies. Rapper Karl Kani was one of the first, launching a line of jeans in 1989. For decades, fashion had subscribed to a sort of trickle down theory—upper-crust designers skimmed lessons from the streets and then sold them back to the people for higher prices. Now the face of fashion was looking more to the people who were originating the styles. And, increasingly, the people who were actually launching the fashion trends were also selling the garments they had inspired.

In the '80s, having a gold chain was a status symbol among some rappers. Now, having one's own fashion line has become the new status symbol. Russell Simmons has Phat Farm, P. Diddy has Sean Jean, the Wu-Tang Clan has Wu-Wear Inc., R&B

singer Sisqó has the Dragon Collection, the Cash Money Millionaires have Cash Money Clothing, Jay-Z and Damon Dash have Rocawear, and Snoop Dogg, OutKast, and many other rappers have their own personal fashion lines.

And the ventures are more than mere vanity affairs. Combs' Sean Jean line, launched in 1999, was expecting sales in 2001 of $8 to $10 million from its underwear and loungewear line alone. And the sales aren't necessarily linked to the popularity of the artist's music. It's about creating a vibe, spinning a fantasy, selling a lifestyle. "Forty percent of our customers don't even know who Sean John is," Jeffrey Tweedy, executive producer of the line, told *USA Today* in August of 2001. "They just like the product."

The success of hip-hoppers has encouraged musicians from other genres to jump into the fashion market. Jennifer Lopez now has a J.Lo line; Santana has a collection of women's shoes and boots that are sold at Macy's stores; and Britney Spears is also testing the waters. Still more musicians, including Destiny's Child, country singer Faith Hill, and hip-hop-soul singer Mary J. Blige, have signed lucrative cosmetics endorsement deals.

When Aaliyah appeared in Tommy Jeans' advertising campaign in Fall of 1995, she helped push forward the hip-hop fashion revolution. She didn't start it, and she didn't finish it, but she helped wage it. Years later, designer Tommy Hilfiger would align himself with Britney Spears (he sponsored her tour) and the Rolling Stones (they even collaborated on a promotional CD). But his alliance with Aaliyah helped set the tone. It was also big money: In 1997, sales of Hilfiger's products reached $661.7 million. In later years, as hip-hoppers launched their own lines, Hilfiger's sales would be challenged. But the lesson for the fashion industry was clear: Hip-hip wasn't just about the street. It was also about Madison Avenue.

Aaliyah's presence in Hilfiger's ads was also a cultural breakthrough. Finally, the face of hip-hop style wasn't a menacing one—and it wasn't a watered-down one either. It was the face of a confident and stylish young teen. Suddenly, more young women were able to locate themselves in the hip-hop movement. Aaliyah, for the campaign, wore baggy jeans and sexy tube tops. She blurred gender lines in a way that was nonconfrontational. On her debut album, Aaliyah performed a song entitled "Young Nation"—her Tommy ads helped display the strength and vibrancy of this youth culture.

In October 2001, I discovered that Aaliyah had a fashion secret. Aaliyah and her friend Kidada Jones were planning to launch their own fashion line. Aaliyah was already famous for being a style-setter and she had been preparing to capitalize on her good taste. But because of Aaliyah's untimely passing, she never launched her line.

Aaliyah's video and fashion work, in life, eventually helped win her roles in Hollywood. As she grew more secure about her looks and her sexuality, her maturity came through on the small screen and Hollywood directors soon got the message as well. "I can't say I had a specific plan," she told *Mixmag.* "From childhood I knew I wanted to be an actress and dancer: a total entertainer. I would sit in a movie theater thinking, 'One day I'll be on that silver screen.' "

She was about to get her chance.

7 | are you that somebody?

> She was a wonderful and talented artist who will be missed by everyone whose lives she touched.
>
> —Jet Li

Remember *Annie*? It's the cute, sweet little story of an orphan girl during a more innocent time period in American history. Of course, it wasn't really a more innocent time; there are no innocent times except in memory. But *Annie* is an endearing, enduring sort of memory, filled with kind millionaire benefactors, singing freckle-faced girls, and the triumph of good over evil. And that, as we've said, was Aaliyah's first experience in show business.

It's a long way from *Annie* to "Akasha." The latter name is the title character of *The Queen of the Damned,* the film which was Aaliyah's last Hollywood experience. Her character was a 6,000-year-old vampire: beautiful, evil, thirsty for blood, passionate and cruel. Near the end of her life, I did an interview with Aaliyah and, when the subject of her daring new role came up, she became noticeably animated. You could tell she delighted in upsetting expectations by taking on such a part; there was a crooked smile on her lips and a naughty gleam in her eye. Her arms waving, and without waiting for encouragement, she went on to describe in delicious, debauched detail one of the sexiest, most sadistic scenes in the movie. One in which she seduces her co-star, Irish actor Stuart Townsend, and, while the two are half-naked in a steamy bath, sucks blood out of his chest.

Harold Guskin, Aaliyah's acting coach, had a front row seat to the young singer's transformation from reserved singer to uninhibited screen star. When I talked to the New York-based acting teacher, he was still shaken by his star pupil's unexpected death, but was eager to discuss her legacy.

Guskin has worked with some of Hollywood's best-known and most respected talents, including Kevin Kline, Glenn Close, and James Gandolfini. Despite all the star power that's passed before his eyes, he still had a clear recollection of the first day he met Aaliyah. She walked through his door in late 1998, looking to study with him. Guskin's acting lessons are demanding, intellectually and emotionally, but, after a few introductory hours, Aaliyah was happily seeing him several times a week.

"You can't survive me unless you're a hard worker," Guskin laughs. "I work with great actors and she fit right in. She was curious and serious. She worked a lot and I was very tough on her. In this field, when you get somebody so nice and lovely you have to take them into places they don't normally go. You take them to the ugly parts, the emotional parts. She never backed off."

Aaliyah's preparation for work as an actress was intriguingly eclectic. In the privacy of Guskin's Manhattan workspace, with Guskin playing the scenes along with her, Aaliyah poured herself into some of the greatest characters, and the greatest works, in the history of drama. She read scenes from Tennessee Williams *The Glass Menagerie,* a play about faded southern belles, madness and the glass-like fragility of private fantasy worlds. Aaliyah also honed her new craft by acting scenes from Anton Chekhov's classic, *The Seagull,* a drama about fame and art, family connections, and romantic longing.

Aaliyah also threw herself into the works of Shakespeare. She took on sections from *Twelfth Night* and *Romeo and Juliet.* Guskin remembers one scene in particular that Aaliyah read through again and again, relishing the language, the poetry, and resonance of the words:

JULIET

Come, night; come, Romeo; come, thou
  day in night;
For thou wilt lie upon the wings of night
Whiter than new snow upon a raven's
  back.
Come, gentle night; come, loving, black-
  brow'd night,
Give me my Romeo; and, when he shall
  die,
Take him and cut him out in little stars,
And he will make the face of heaven so fine
That all the world will be in love with night
And pay no worship to the garish sun

Guskin says one of Aaliyah's greatest gifts was her ability not only to sing music, but also to speak music. When she was reciting lines—Shakespeare or Tennessee Williams, Chekhov or a Hollywood script—she would unlock the rhythm of the words, find the beat of the language, and make whatever passage she was reading more melodious, more fluid. "She was very musical in the way that an actor has to have," says Guskin. "She could play the lines and let them take her wherever they had to go."

There is music in language—in the greatest stage dramas, in the highest quality screenplays. Musicians, however, don't typically make the best actors.

In fact, they generally make pretty lousy ones. There's an inverse relationship between pop stardom and acting talent: the bigger the pop star, the worse they usually are as actors. Bob Dylan, arguably the greatest lyricist in the history of American popular music, appeared in the 1987 movie *Hearts of Fire;* if you log on to the International Movie Database on the Web (www.imdb.com), you'll find that, at last count, a democratic survey of viewers gave the film a grand total of 2.6 stars out of 10.

Madonna is arguably the biggest female pop star in American history. She's made over a dozen films; she acted well in only one of them. *A League of Their Own* was good despite the Material Girl (not that her part was that big anyway) and the same is true of the Woody Allen comedy *Shadows and Fog* (Madonna's part is a glorified cameo). Pretty much every other film she's made has been a box office or critical failure, including *Shanghai Surprise* (which nearly killed the career of her co-star and then-husband, Sean Penn), *A Certain Sacrifice,* and *The Next Best Thing* (a romantic comedy critics felt lacked both romance and comedy). Madonna was quite good in *Desperately Seeking Susan,* but that was back in 1985 when her acting was natural and unselfconscious. It was also her first big film.

Interestingly, two subsets of musicians have fared rather well when it comes to crossing over from music to films. The first is R&B divas. The great jazz singer Billie Holiday appeared in several films at a time when African American actresses weren't welcome in Hollywood. Of course, judging from the number of above-the-title-parts in good movies that African American actresses get in Hollywood even today, they still don't seem all that welcome. But pop music stardom has been one way for African-American singers to open Tinseltown's doors. In the '70s, Diana Ross starred in three film classics: *Lady Sings the Blues*, *Mahogany*, and *The Wiz*. Yeah, sure she was too old to play the lead role of Dorothy in that last one, but the music and dancing and general mood were absorbing. Whitney Houston also went from pop star to movie star with her hit movies *The Bodyguard* (1992) and *Waiting to Exhale* (1995).

Most musicians have trouble with words stripped of music because they need music to express themselves. Without instrumentation, they're lost; they can't find the melody in what they're saying, they lose the rhythm and, with it, the emotion and the meaning. Divas, on the other hand, those glamorous, imperious singers who are known by a single name—the Billies, the Dianas, the Whitneys—are already playing a part. Part of being a diva is bringing the pain, bringing the drama, whether you're onstage or offstage; part of being a diva is moving with a theatrical air about you; part of being a diva is seeming so much bigger than life you that you appear to be projected onto a movie. So for a diva-in-training like Aaliyah, moving from stage to screen wasn't that big a jump. Her life had prepared her for it. "Some of it is me, some of it's not. But you never really know," Aaliyah once said of her offstage persona. "I don't think I do sometimes."

The other group of musicians that tends to do well in the world of film is hip-hoppers. Will Smith (*Independence Day, Men in Black, Ali*) is one of the biggest stars in Hollywood. LL Cool J has had a bigger career as a character actor in Hollywood than he has as a rapper, the field in which he first made his name. How many LL Cool J albums do you own? Probably none, and if you do have a copy, it's probably one of his earlier, better albums. How many LL Cool J albums can you even name? But most people have seen one or two, or at least heard of, LL Cool J's last couple of films: *Charlie's Angels, Any Given Sunday, In Too Deep,* and *Deep Blue Sea.* Snoop Dogg, Ja Rule, P. Diddy, Mos Def, Queen Latifah, and too many other rappers to name have also carved out booming, or at least semi-booming, film careers. Many are doing better at the box office than they are in record stores.

Hip-hop soul singers are following suit. Erykah Badu was quite good in *The Cider House Rules.* And the great Lauryn Hill was radiant co-starring alongside Whoopi Goldberg in *Sister Act 2: Back in the*

Habit (1993), graceful in the arthouse flick *King of the Hill* (1993), and striking and effective in the little-seen, small-budget production *Restaurant* (1998). The reason that performers with roots in hip-hop are so effective as thespians is perhaps because hip-hop, at its root, is about talking. Hip-hop is the music of language. Even without beats, hip-hop stars are able to bring out the music of words. Also, hip-hop, as an art form, came into being around the same time that music videos became popular. Being a rap star has long been linked to being a visual star—to having the right look, a cool posture, having the emotion of one's words spill out onto one's face in a way that viewers can see, feel and identify with. Aaliyah knew that world, she came up in it. Her style of singing, with its smooth conversational contours, was, at times, closer to rap than to standard gospel-influenced pop soul. So when it came to acting, like any other child of hip-hop, Aaliyah was good to go.

Aaliyah and Hollywood courted each other carefully, and over a number of years. It was like one of those romances where the two lovers are friends first before they realize, after much time has passed, that there are deeper feelings, and stronger forces, at work.

The flirting came first. Aaliyah's relationship with Hollywood started with the Keenan Ivory Wayans comedy *A Low Down Dirty Shame* (1994); she contributed a performance of the song "The Thing I Like." The movie was quite good, but the project was somewhat low-profile. Her next movie soundtrack contribution was to the 20th Century Fox animated film *Anastasia*. The film is a fictionalized take on the real-life mystery of what happened to the daughter of the Czar of Russia after the Russian Revolution. The film garnered mixed reviews, but Aaliyah's song, the ballad "Journey to the Past," was a substantial hit.

"Journey to the Past" was nominated for an Academy Award for Best Song and, as a result, Aaliyah was invited to perform the song at the 1998 Oscars. It was a major moment in her life; she got to dress up and rub shoulders with the likes of Russell Crowe (nominated that year for his star turn in *L.A. Confidential*), and Ben Affleck (up for writing, along with Matt Damon, the screenplay for *Good Will Hunting*). Unfortunately, that was also the year that *Titanic* was nominated for pretty much every prize but Best Foreign Film and "Journey to the Past" was brushed aside in a *Titanic* sweep of most of the top awards. Celine Dion's "My Heart Will Go On," the theme from *Titanic* (written by James Horner) ended up winning the Oscar for Best Song.

Despite the loss, it was a satisfying night for Aaliyah. After all, she had gone to the Oscars, arguably the biggest and brightest of all entertainment awards shows, and it was a relatively eventful edition of the annual ceremony. Aaliyah would have seen hubris: Dion pounding her chest during her rendition of that *Titanic* song, and James Cameron declaring "I'm the King of the World!" as he clutched his just-won statuette for Best Director. She would have seen glamour: Susan Sarandon clad in Dolce & Gabbana, Helena Bonham Carter in Deborah Milner, Meg Ryan in Vera Wang. Aaliyah would also have seen pure, naked, unmistakable star power: Madonna chatting with Joni Mitchell, Jennifer Lopez with her then-beau Sean "Puffy" Combs, Jack Nicholson slyly picking up yet another Best Actor award, this time for his role in the comedy *As Good As It Gets* in which he appeared opposite Helen Hunt, who also won that night for Best Actress. In short, Aaliyah would have seen everything she wanted to be, everything she was building towards—and a few things she was trying to avoid. Said Aaliyah: "As I was walking down the carpet [at the 1998 Oscars], all these people kept telling me it was going to be the most-watched Oscars ever which didn't help. Michael Bolton was singing after me and we were both backstage going, 'God, are you as nervous as I am?' It was a hell of an experience."

Despite all the excess and all the high fashion, Aaliyah made the coolest fashion statement of the night: She wore a simple black gown that she had purchased off the rack at a mall outside of Detroit.

Denise Davis-Cotton, Aaliyah's high school principal, was watching on television. "That was the first time I had one of my emotional moments about Aaliyah," she said. "It was when she sang on the Academy Awards. I was home watching it. I cried like I was her mother. It hit me at that time that this student had realized a dream. She had matriculated from a school for the fine and performing arts and fulfilled her goal and achieved her mission. I was overwhelmed with joy and gratitude."

Aaliyah scored again in 1999 with the hit song "Are You That Somebody?" off the soundtrack to the Eddie Murphy comedy *Dr. Doolittle.* While the song wasn't nominated for an Academy Award it was a huge hit on radio. Its stuttering rhythms and smooth vocals reminded listeners why they had fallen in love with Aaliyah's style to begin with. The song, produced by Timbaland, was a honed, mature version of Aaliyah's signature sound: cool, crisp, and confident.

Aaliyah's flirtation with Hollywood finally resulted in her cinematic first date: a role in the action film *Romeo Must Die* in 2000. The action film was directed by Andrzej Bartkowiak, a little-known filmmaker who had also worked on such high-profile hits as *Terms of Endearment, Prizzi's Honor* and *The Devil's Advocate,* although he worked on those films only as a cinematographer. *Romeo Must Die* was Bartkowiak's first film as a director; he would later go on to direct *Exit Wounds* starring DMX.

But the main attraction of *Romeo Must Die* wasn't its director; it was Aaliyah and her co-star, martial arts action icon Jet Li. Li had made a big impression in *Lethal Weapon 4* in 1998; he was already a huge star throughout the Asian world. Aaliyah was recruited to star in *Romeo Must Die* in part for her singing. Said Aaliyah: "We actually talked about the soundtrack before we even shot the movie." She eventually took the role of "Trish O'Day," the daughter of a business-like, family-oriented gangster, in part because she liked the toughness of the character, who was rebelling against her father's criminal ways. Said Aaliyah: "I love Trish. I think she's the bomb. She's sexy, she's tough, and she's got attitude."

She soon came to admire her co-star Li as well. Li, who was born in Beijing, China, was already a veteran of some two dozen films from his homeland and Hong Kong and, by watching him, Aaliyah learned a few lessons about preparation and professionalism. The film's action scenes were designed by martial-arts expert Corey Yuen, and, in one of them, Aaliyah got to fight alongside Li, or rather, Li got to fight using her as a human weapon, doing battle with a villain by swinging Aaliyah around. "I rehearsed that scene with Corey for a month," Aaliyah said soon after the film was released. "But Jet and I didn't hook up until the day we shot. That's how dope he is; he doesn't have to rehearse. He just comes to the set and fights."

Although *Romeo Must Die* was an action film, it had some emotional moments as well and Aaliyah got to put some of her new acting skills to use. She refused to use any chemicals or artificial means to cry on camera, like blowing menthol up her nose or putting fake tears on her cheeks; she insisted on doing it for real. "When I had to do my crying scene . . . man! I had to deal with a lot of pain and emotion to bring the tears up," Aaliyah said to *Blues & Soul* magazine in 2000. "That was the most intimidating part of the whole script. My grandmother passed two years ago and I was very close with her, so I thought about her a lot and other painful moments in my life. It was a very depressing, draining day. When I see it now, it's very rewarding to know that I actually did cry and the tears were very real."

Romeo Must Die was a solid hit at the box office and an impressive performer on DVD as well. The experience prepared Aaliyah well for what would be the biggest challenge of her career.

8 | the queen of the damned

She was so good at manipulating her image in photographs and videos and in film. But dealing with her on a day to day basis, she was completely without artifice.

—Michael Rymer, director, *The Queen of the Damned*

People can get obsessive about the books they love. That's a good thing. *The Queen of the Damned* the movie, was based on a book of the same name by horror writer Anne Rice, the same author who wrote *Interview With a Vampire.* Rice, of course, has legions of fussy, obsessed fans who are protective of her work and have encyclopedic knowledge about her characters, her descriptions, and all the little ins and outs of the vampire–filled universe which she has created. Around the same time that *The Queen of the Damned* geared up to go into production, two other major works of fantasy, *The Fellowship of the Ring* (based on the series by

J.R.R. Tolkien) and *Harry Potter and the Sorcerer's Stone* (based on the children's books by J.K. Rowling) were also making their way to the big screen. The Tolkien and Potter adaptations put the word out to watchful, anxious fans that they were making movies that would be dutifully faithful to the original texts. The filmmakers behind *The Queen of the Damned,* however, planned to live dangerously.

A bad movie adaptation can be worse than a bad cover song. When some no-talent destroys a classic song, there's an easy solution for any offended listener: Slide the original into the CD player or download it off the Web and let the bad new version wash away. With a bad adaptation of a book, however, the situation is somewhat different. When we read a book we create our own images of the characters, of the setting, how it looks, the colors, the textures. Once we see a movie, it's hard to hold on to those original images. Cinema can be stronger than the imagination and even re-reading the book in question can't free us from the tyranny of its vision. The James Bond movies were based on a fictional character from the printed page. But when most people think of Bond, the ideas in their head come not from the printed page, but from the series of actors who have portrayed him on screen, from Sean Connery to Pierce Brosnan.

So Michael Rymer, the Melbourne, Australia-born director of *The Queen of the Damned* had his work cut out for him as he began to bring the Anne Rice book to life as a movie. The first Anne Rice book that was brought to the big screen, *Interview with a Vampire,* starred Brad Pitt as the vampire "Louis de Point du Lac" and Tom Cruise as "Lestat de Lioncourt." In the new movie, "Lestat" is played by Irish actor Stuart Townsend and Aaliyah plays his opposite, "Akasha." The basic plot is this: "Lestat" has remade himself into a rock star, and his music ends up awakening the queen of all vampires, "Akasha." It's a gothic thriller, one that could be either effective or ridiculous, depending on the skill of the actors and the talent of the director. Rymer came into the project with a slim resumé: Before *Queen of the Damned,* he had directed just four previous movies, all low budget, including the well-received indie drama *Angel Baby* (about two schizophrenics who meet in therapy and fall wildly in love) and the effective urban crime thriller *In Too Deep* (where perhaps Rymer first learned to work with hip-hop actors).

The first problem Rymer faced was casting. The part of "Akasha" called for someone who was beautiful and strong and who had the ability to project unblinking wickedness. "Akasha" is a timeless, deathless beauty with the power to make men's heads explode and create fear even in the cold hearts of vampires. Some babe from a UPN sitcom wouldn't do, and neither would some soft dame from the British indie filmmaking world. To give you an idea, here's one scene from the book:

"Akasha turned full circle, her garments caught in a brief dance of black and white silk all around her; and everywhere human beings were caught as if by invisible hands and flung to the floor," Anne Rice writes. "Their bodies went into convulsions. The women, looking down at the stricken victims, wailed and tore their hair. . . . It took me a moment to realize what was happening, that she was killing the men. It wasn't fire. It was some invisible attack upon the vital organs. . . . Then I heard her voice inside my head: *Kill them Lestat. Slaughter the males to the last one.*"

When I talked to Rymer in September of 2001, he was overseeing the final edit of his movie and was still very much caught up in the issues of its production. "That was exactly the toughest part," Rymer said about the casting process. "The idea of who am I gonna get to play this role? Some older woman with a deeper voice? Is that gonna make it scarier?"

While thinking about the issue of casting, Rymer had a bit of a revelation. "I came to this conclusion: Trying to make a vampire film, I really wanted to explore why vampires are interesting to us today. Well,

aaliyah strikes a pose in New York City on May 9, 2001.

PHOTOGRAPHER JIM COOPER. AP/WORLD WIDE PHOTOS.

Making an arrival at the Essence Awards on April 27, 2001. PHOTOGRAPHER DARLA KHAZEI. AP/WORLD WIDE PHOTOS.

With co-star Jet Li at the world premiere of their movie *Romeo Must Die* on March 20, 2000, in Los Angeles.
PHOTOGRAPHER RENE MACURA. AP/WORLD WIDE PHOTOS.

taking in a screening of *The Others* in New York City on August 2, 2001.
PHOTOGRAPHER TINA FINEBURG. AP/WORLD WIDE PHOTOS.

aaliyah as Queen Akasha, a 6,000-year-old Egyptian vampire, in *The Queen of the Damned*, a movie based on the novel by Anne Rice.

aaliyah as Queen Akasha, with co-star Stuart Townsend as the vampire Lestat, in *The Queen of the Damned.*

the wreckage of Aaliyah's plane, which crashed into a swamp on the western end of the Marsh Harbour Airport in the Bahamas on August 25, 2001.
PHOTOGRAPHER TIM AYLEN.AP/WORLD WIDE PHOTOS.

the singer's funeral hearse making its way through the streets of Manhattan on August 31, 2001.
PHOTOGRAPHER PAUL HAWTHORNE. AP/WORLD WIDE PHOTOS.

aaliyah's mother, Diane Haughton, center right, holds hands with Aaliyah's brother, Rashad, as they leave the Frank E. Campbell Funeral Chapel on August 31, 2001; the singer's boyfriend, Damon Dash, is behind in the center. PHOTOGRAPHER STEPHEN CHERNIN. AP/WORLD WIDE PHOTOS.

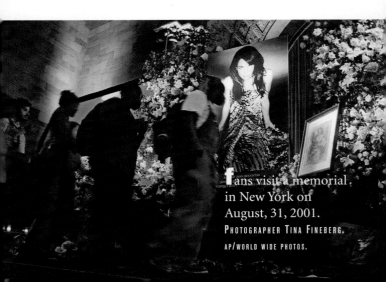

fans visit a memorial in New York on August, 31, 2001. PHOTOGRAPHER TINA FINEBERG. AP/WORLD WIDE PHOTOS.

Paying tribute on Sunset Boulevard in West Hollywood, California.

PHOTOGRAPHER KEVORK DJANSEZIAN. AP/WORLD WIDE PHOTOS.

a vampire is immortal, all-powerful, and usually very sexy. The sexuality is half the job of being a vampire. I had seen Aaliyah's videos and she is incredibly slinky and sensuous and very charismatic. I was sort of gambling on the concept that the more sexy Aaliyah played the character, the more powerful she would be."

Starting out, the biggest problem was that Rymer had no idea who Aaliyah was. He had heard the name bandied about, and Aaliyah's name did enter the mix of the many actresses who were being considered for the plum role. Then, one day, Rymer found himself talking with actor Willem Dafoe *(Platoon, The English Patient)* when her name came up. "The first person who really told me about her was Willem Dafoe," says Rymer. "I was chatting with him about *The Queen of the Damned* and he was interested in a role. And I said, 'Yeah, and we're talking to Aaliyah about playing "Akasha," the queen of the damned.' And he said, 'Oh Aaliyah's amazing!' And I said, 'You know Aaliyah?' And he said, 'Yeah, my [son] is a huge fan, I know all about her—she's amazing!' So she came highly recommended from the beginning."

Rymer's first encounter with Aaliyah was somewhat rocky—or rather it was unnervingly smooth for the high-spirited Aussie filmmaker. Aaliyah, along with her mother Diane and her brother

Rashad, flew to Los Angeles to meet with Rymer about the movie. Aaliyah and her family were staying at the hip, luxurious Nikko Hotel and Rymer met them in the lobby. Says Rymer: "When I ended up working with them and knowing them for a year, I thought Aaliyah was the sweetest, kindest person I'd ever met. A very spiritually advanced sort of soul. And I think that also applied to Diane and Rashad. But when I first met them I thought they were weird. I thought: 'there's something wrong with these people.' "

Why? Continues Rymer: "Well, because they just sat there so calmly. It was almost outside of human behavior. I wanted to get a reaction out of them. But you couldn't faze them about anything. You couldn't get them upset or excited. They were just sort of even-tempered and straightforward and simple about how they dealt with things."

So Rymer talked tough. He wanted Aaliyah to know what a difficult challenge awaited her. If she tried to play a vampire and failed, she could look ridiculous, she could ruin the film and damage her career. Sure, she had done *Romeo Must Die.* Sure, that film had made some money and gotten some good reviews. But in *Romeo* she was playing a human being, and a human being very much like herself: young, stylish, outgoing. Her chief problem in that part was just trying to not look awkward, to succeed in acting natural. Now, with *Queen of the Damned,* she would have to act supernatural—and that was a far more daunting task.

So Rymer tried to scare her a bit, to shake her up, to see how much pressure she could take right off the bat. "You're asking a twenty-one-year-old girl to play the most powerful, evil creature in the world. That's a serious acting challenge. That's a dive with the highest degree of difficulty. She can't just come in and think she's just gonna show up on the set and make this work.

"I was prepared to consider her but she was gonna have to work her ass off with an acting coach and a movement coach and a dialect coach to make this work. And if she's not prepared to do that she was wasting everyone's time. I said all this to her the first time I met her. I said, 'If you're not prepared to do all that, you're gonna make a fool of yourself and you're gonna fail. This is a dangerous part.' "

So how did Aaliyah react? Rymer laughs. "She said 'No problem,' " says Rymer. "She said 'What do I do and who with and when do I start?' Not even worried about it."

Rymer, however, had one more test for his young star. He asked her to prepare a reading from the Oscar Wilde play *Salome.* The play's script is wordy and dense, and the title character is complex and re-vengeful. "It was the meanest thing I could have done," says Rymer, laughing again. "The selection was 10 pages long, dense with dialogue, really complicated, flowery, poetic dialogue."

Aaliyah's training with her acting coach, however, had prepared her well. Rymer was surprised and impressed with her reading. "It was quite a good scene for a potential 'Akasha,' " says Rymer. "She did it well because of her training as a dancer and a musician. She knows how to use her body very well, she had a natural physicality. When she started getting into that whole feline energy thing—it was exciting."

The part of Akasha was just perfect for Aaliyah at that stage of her career. Her image was, as she liked to put it, "street but sweet," and her music had a tough core with soft edges. Akasha allowed her to explore her secret places, the alleyways of emotion she had never revealed to her fans, her family, or even to herself. "I've always been mysterious," Aaliyah once told *Vibe.* "My mother and my father always used to ask me, 'What are you thinking about, what's going on?' There are times I don't understand myself, you know what I mean?" Aaliyah went on to add: "I have black-out shades in my apartment. I push a button, it's totally dark. I think I'm a bit of a vampire in real life, and there are times when I just want to be myself. I wanna be alone."

Aaliyah's new character was also Egyptian, and Egypt was a country that had fascinated the young singer for years. Aaliyah also found herself drawn to her new character's strength and brazen sexuality. It allowed her to project an image that was bolder than any she had revealed in the past. Said Aaliyah: "She's very evil, extremely powerful, and she's a bit of a brat because she's so young. She's used to getting what she wants. So it was a real challenge for me to play all those sides to her. This was the first time I had to do a little love scene which I was very nervous about." She continued: "However, as a character she's very manipulative and very sexual so I had to put my shyness to one side and just be the character. In the movie, the love scene took place in a hot tub filled with roses. Once I got over the shy part, it was a lot of fun."

The Queen of the Damned was filmed in and around Melbourne, Australia. The first scene Aaliyah shot was a striking one. Her character goes into a vampire bar, flirts outrageously with some of the patrons, ends up ripping one poor guy's heart out, and then goes on to incinerate the rest of the clientele. Afterwards, Aaliyah's character struts away, happy and satisfied with the mayhem she has just brought about. "It's a very cool scene," says Rymer. "What I remember about that day is all the extras and the crew saying 'That girl's amazing.' We had a lot of fun that first day. I was very proud to have such a talented person playing the villain."

Rymer was struck by the balance of his young star and how close she was to her family. Aaliyah was simultaneously shooting the movie and recording tracks for a new album—a scheduling challenge even for an entertainment veteran, let alone a semi-newcomer like Aaliyah. She would shoot scenes by night (the time of vampires) and, by day, she would break character and lay down vocals for the album that would be her third and best release, the self-titled *Aaliyah.* Sometimes she would film all day and all night. The signs of the pressure she was under weren't readily apparent, in part, perhaps, because of the support of her family.

"Diane and her family took care of Aaliyah very well," says Rymer. "They gave her anything she needed. She was never distracted by the usual b.s. that comes with this business. That's a powerful thing for an actor—if you can focus on what's important, it's a great asset."

Rymer remembers fondly that, despite her hectic schedule, Aaliyah used to drop by the set on her days off just to say hi. Says Rymer: "When I think of Aaliyah, I think of this girl in low-cut jeans looking sexy and casual and dropping by to say hello."

Aaliyah's cousin, Jomo Hankerson, told me there was initially some hesitation at Blackground Records about recording an album in Australia. The crew he had assembled for the project worried that

Melbourne was too far away and would lack the excitement that they had grown accustomed to in New York City. "When I had to tell the creative team that we had to go to Australia to finish recording the album, nobody was excited about the 24-hour flight," said Jomo. "I had to bribe everybody with business fare tickets in order to get them on the plane. It was really like flying off into the unknown."

The recording was mostly handled at Sing Sing Studios in Melbourne. Jomo said that, as it turned out, Aaliyah and the rest of her team found Melbourne a city that combined the best of everything: The studio itself was up-to-date and modern, the city offered a number of cool restaurants and nightclubs, and the people had a small-town, affable attitude. "I think what made the vibe so incredible was how wrong we were and how far off our expectations were once we got there. Melbourne was incredible. The people were incredible. We had a lot of fun in the studio and outside of it. Aaliyah was down there and was having a lot of fun although she was working hard shooting the movie. She was up at 4 A.M. getting makeup, shooting all day until 6 P.M. and coming into the studio at 7 P.M. and working all night until 11 or 12 P.M. at night. It was tough, but she got into this zone that creative people sometimes get in. We were all down there zoning."

Sometimes actors need to reach deep down into themselves to find a place that is not so nice in order to create a character that's interesting and rich. Certainly the character of "Akasha" called for such an exploration. Says Guskin, Aaliyah's acting coach: "I think the biggest problem she had was that she was a sweet, shy person. She was shy about going to some of the places I asked her to go—angry and tough and emotionally deep places."

In the end, Rymer says, Aaliyah was able to find those places. And he says her last scene, since her passing, has taken on an unexpected emotional dimension. In the scene, Aaliyah's character is in statue form. The makeup artists painted her all alabaster to give her the appearance of something made of stone. The process took three hours. The cast and crew gasped when Aaliyah came onto the set. She looked like some mythic creature. Even her eyes were covered with alabaster contacts (which, according to Rymer, were extremely painful to wear). Without a word, as silent as the statue she was playing, Aaliyah took her place on the set. Later, with the addition of special effects, her stone body would seem to crumble into dust. The last scene Aaliyah shot for *The Queen of the Damned*, ironically, was a death scene.

Says Rymer: "She does have a death scene. It's very beautiful. It is sort of eerie to watch now. There is certainly a poignancy about it that was added to it by the events of real life."

"Akasha" was a tragic character, a creature filled with unquenchable passion and incapable of real love. Aaliyah, who had searched for romance her entire life, finally found it in an unexpected place, with an unexpected man.

9 | aaliyah and damon: a love story

> She was my best friend and will remain in my heart forever.
>
> —Damon Dash, Aaliyah's boyfriend

When Aaliyah and Damon Dash first hooked up, neither of them could have known that she would only have about a year more to live.

Aaliyah knew dating was difficult, and that when you're a celebrity relationships have their own particular problems. Celebrities seem to break up faster and get divorced quicker than regular folks. Mariah Carey, Whitney Houston, Jennifer Lopez, and too many other singers have had very public break-ups and make-ups, love spats and other episodes of romantic turmoil. Most fans only learned that Janet Jackson had been married when word leaked out she was getting a divorce. It's a common ritual:

Whenever a celebrity gets married or engaged, ordinary folks make informal bets on how long the relationship will last. Typically, celebrity pairings seem destined to last about as long as the average toothbrush. One wonders why many actors, singers, and other entertainers get married at all.

Although celebrities like to complain how hard it is to date when you're in the public eye, the truth is it's much more difficult for ordinary people. Ordinary people can't whisk their dates off to the South of France for a weekend. Ordinary people can't give six-karat diamonds as get-to-know-you gifts. Ordinary people aren't invited to all the glamorous functions and upscale parties that celebrities routinely get to bring their dates to. And ordinary people, unlike celebrities, aren't propositioned by millions of adoring fans everyday. In their fantasies, perhaps, but not in real life.

But celebrity relationships do have their problems and Aaliyah had experienced some of them first hand. Aaliyah told *The Mirror* (London): "When I first got into the business I lost a lot of friends. People kind of fell out because they couldn't deal with it or understand it." She added that virtually all of her new friends were in the entertainment business: "They're just like me and understand it." The episode with R.Kelly had left her hurt and a little vulnerable. In its aftermath, she was more wary of the press than ever and was cautious about giving out any information about her love life. After R.Kelly, her relationships would all be stealth relationships; they would fly beneath the radar and only her close friends would know about them. Aaliyah didn't want the spotlight to ruin something that was personal and private. She was almost never linked to anyone in the paper or in gossip magazines. She was almost never seen out on the town with anyone other than her girlfriends. Whatever she was doing she was keeping it on the down low.

But whether she was dating or not, Aaliyah liked to advertise herself as available. She told *Mademoiselle* in April of 2000, "Hey, I haven't been out on a date in a year! Mostly, I'll just do dinner with my best friend, Kidada Jones, or hang out at clubs like Lotus with my fashion girls. But lately I've been spending all my time recording or filming. And with *The Matrix* sequels coming up . . ." Ultimately the message was this: Yes she was single. No, don't give her a call because she's way too busy to date. Plus, Aaliyah seemed to value her alone time. She told a reporter in October of 2000: "I like to keep by myself. Being in this business means 90 percent of your life is public so that side of my life is for me. I've never really had a boyfriend and I don't have one now but when I do I will try my best to keep what we do just for me."

Aaliyah did enjoy hanging around New York. She

had a place on Central Park West and she was a fixture of the city's nightlife. "I love it!" she told *Blues & Soul* magazine. "New York has its own energy. Sure people come up to me in the street and say they admire my work or whatever. I love being in the heart of it all—to be able to walk out of my apartment and go get a bagel or go shopping. I may have to get a place in L.A. at some point and be bi-coastal because of the film thing, but this is home to me. I was born here and have a lot of friends here. Essentially . . . I'm a New York kinda girl."

Aaliyah had also become a New York kind of artist. New York is a city with all kinds of musical scenes: hip-hop and punk, alt-country and reggae, dance music and jazz. In her later interviews, Aaliyah began to express her interest in a broader range of musical styles and artists. For example, she loved Trent Reznor of the art-noise act Nine Inch Nails. The sound of Nine Inch Nails was worlds away from Aaliyah's softer, earlier work, but it was an indication of her broadening tastes. "I think Trent Reznor's dope," she told London's *Daily Telegraph*. "His sounds and melodies are ridiculous. That last album's just sick!" (She meant all this in a good way, by the way.) She was a true child of hip-hop—ever-curious, ever-exploring, looking to sample the world around her.

And, for a princess of hip-hop, she was in New York City at the right musical moment. Around the year 2000, the music world centered around New York City was taken over by a new kind of executive: the hip-hop mogul. Young, or at least youngish, African American men in the music industry were getting paid like never before. In the days before hip-hop, the music industry had a (deserved) rep for ripping off artists, for leaving them broke and broken, with only memories of greatness and happy times to sustain them. It's hard to name a blues musician who had a reputation as a mogul. It's hard to name a Black rock and roller who is famous for all the money he has stored away. Instead, Black music history is a story of bankruptcies and financial collapses. Billie Holiday was always hurting for money. Jimi Hendrix spent the last few years of his life in a severe money crunch. Members of the singing trio TLC, an act that sold millions of albums worldwide, once told me that at one stage they were so broke that the lights in their homes were turned off.

During the age of hip-hop, some Blacks finally moved into the boardroom—or rather, they forced their way in. They certainly weren't invited in. Of course, Berry Gordy had enjoyed tremendous success as the head of Motown in the '60s and '70s, but few African American executives were able to follow his lead. Major labels didn't quite get hip-hop, didn't quite know how to market it. Music industry suits tried to ignore it in the '70s, then they kind of hoped it would go the way of the Pet Rock in the '80s, and in the '90s they decided if hip-hop was going to be around to stay, they might as well try and make some money off of it. To harness the new music's power, the major labels were obliged to sign deals with smaller, streetier labels that knew the territory—outfits like Death Row records and So So Def and Def Jam and Bad Boy. The young Black owners of these smaller outfits became powerbrokers in the process—and some ended up running major labels themselves.

First there was Russell Simmons, the original hip-hop mogul, the godfather of hip-hop, and the co-founder of Def Jam Records. By some estimates, he was worth more than $200 million in 2001. Russell started out as a concert promoter in the '80s. He has since branched out into fashion and other ventures: His Phat Farm clothing company went from gross revenues of $60 million in 1999 to $150 million in 2000. He was also a fixture on the party scene; if there was a major musical event in New York City—rock, rap, or pop—Simmons was likely to be there, dressed casually in jeans, sneakers, and a baseball cap no matter how fancy the occasion. Pundits began to turn to him as the voice of hip-hop, and he appeared in *TIME*, on Nightline, and in *The New York Times.* Before Russell Simmons, hip-hop was all about gold chains and big cars. Simmons showed there was another way to display a sense of power and wealth. He was so laid back in every situation, so seemingly comfortable, he just projected financial security. A brother had to have bank to seem that relaxed at all times. He didn't have to flaunt it because everyone knew that he had it.

Then there was Puff Daddy, P. Diddy, Puffy, Sean Combs—whatever you wanted to call him. He kept changing his name, but he remained a cultural fixture. But by whatever name, and whatever you thought of his music, he was a mogul with a thriving record label (Bad Boy), a clothing empire, and a booming career as a music producer. He started out producing hip-hop/soul singer Mary J. Blige, and he was a key influence on her early, classic hip-hop/soul sound. He was also the Notorious B.I.G.'s chief collaborator and, along with Biggie, he helped create a new vision of hip-hop: still rooted to the street, but with visions of taking that same street culture to corporate boardrooms, upscale clubs, and high society. Puffy showcased a vision of gangsta fabulousness in his lyrics and in his videos, and then went about making it all come true in real life. Everyone—whites and blacks, young and old, the hip and the clueless—wanted to go to his parties at the Hamptons. Everybody wanted to hang with him, whether they liked his music or not. I attended one of his birthday parties and it was one of the most lavish affairs I had ever witnessed, complete with dancing girls in cages and plenty of celebrity guests, from Kevin Costner to Denzel Washington to Donald Trump. It seemed, in the heyday of Puffy, in the mid-'90s, that his star was sure to fall, that there was no way he could maintain that level of stardom. But although his solo work isn't selling like it once did, he continues, into the 21st century, to be a powerful celebrity presence. He's still landing magazine covers, still getting good seats at awards shows, and still getting heavy video play on television.

Damon Dash, CEO of Roc-a-Fella records, was one of the hottest and youngest of the new breed of hip-hop moguls. "I'm a millionaire after taxes," he once boasted to *Black Enterprise* magazine. Dash was open about his connection to the streets, but a little less talkative about his connection to bourgeois society. He often bragged of being raised on the rough streets of Harlem, but he was far less likely to mention the fact that his protective mother made sure he attended boarding school. When his mother died when he was just 16 years old, Dash lost all direction in his life and began running with ne'er do wells in the street. But then one day his cousin, Darien, took him to a music industry party for the rapper/record executive Heavy D. Damon looked around and saw money, success, influence—and it was all legal and above board. A wide-eyed Damon wanted in. Dash told *XXL:* "I was like 'Look at these niggas buying all this champagne and they got all this bitches and they ain't putting in half the work I was putting in on the streets.'"

Soon Dash began to manage music acts, and then he set his sights on starting a label. Roc-a-Fella Records was launched in 1995 by rapper Jay-Z, Dash, and Kareem "Biggs" Burke. Jay-Z was a rapper with a following in the underground, but he was looking to break out. Earlier in 1995, he had returned to the street life but, after being shot at close range, he wisely decided to focus on hip-hop. "It wasn't specifically one thing," he told *The Washington Post.* "It was more so out of fear. You can't run the streets forever. What are you going to be doing when you're 30 years old, or 35 or 40? I had a fear of being nothing—that pretty much drove me." However, Jay-Z had trouble getting the major labels interested in his style of lyrically dense gangsta rap. He told *The New Yorker* that his songs were too "sophisticated" for mainstream record labels. "You had to really like rap to be, like, 'This dude's clever; the way he's using his words, the way he tackles subjects—that's different.' " Interestingly, at one point Jay-Z was a good-natured, attentive grade school student. "He's a very dear kid," Renee Rosenblum-Lowden, his 6th-grade teacher, once told *People.* "There is so much more to him than a person who sings about bitches and 'ho's.' Gee I hope I'm not killing his image."

The major labels didn't seem interested in hooking up with Roc-a-Fella, so the company signed a distribution deal with Priority and put out Jay-Z's first full-length CD, *Reasonable Doubt.* The album was a huge success, critically and commercially. Soon these same major labels were seeking out Dash and Co. looking to make a deal. But the new lords of Roc-a-Fella wanted to be cautious. Jay-Z didn't just want to sign with anybody; he was looking to make a major move. "When everybody else was doing gold," he says, "I was, like, 'I want something platinum.' " Dash was also looking for a lucrative deal, but one that would pay off in the long-term as well. "When record companies were first courting us, they came to me with the nigga deal where they make you think you own a label and you really don't," Dash once said. "I wanted a joint venture because I knew I was going to be successful and the equity would be worth something down the line." In the end, Dash signed a 50–50 deal with Def Jam in which Roc-a-Fella owns half the masters. He had the control he wanted and the type of power that had eluded generations of African Americans in the music industry for years.

Jay-Z has gone on to be one of the most popular gangsta rappers in hip-hop. His lyrics are rude and playful, but often clever. He raps about street life, but his songs also function as carefully observed verbal documentaries of his life, from his run-ins with the law, to the parties he attends, to his ever-growing fame. His music can be macho, rough, and earthy, but he has a pleasant, good-natured delivery that softens his lyrical attack and makes even his hardest-hitting work seem affable. Oddly enough, like Aaliyah, Jay-Z turned out to have soft spot for the musical *Annie*. One of his biggest hit songs, "Hard Knock Life," samples from *Annie* in its chorus. Jay-Z, who has a sister named Annie, first heard the song when he was growing up. "You live in Marcy Projects, Brooklyn, New York, you don't have much," he once told a reporter. "And then you see someone on TV—they don't have much, they're an orphan, and then they get to live in a big mansion. . . . You're gonna take that story. That's something you wish could happen to you. Know what I'm saying? . . . It was just so perfect for me, and it was, 'Yeah I gotta do it. I don't care how hard I fall on my face, but I need to do this record.' "

Meanwhile, Dash took the same aggressive marketing position that he had with the major labels with New York City-based Comet, a company that was interested in distributing Roc-a-Fella's clothing line. Says Dash: "I came in with the same concept I had when I did my joint venture. I'm not licensing to you, I want to own half the company . . . I may not know how to manufacture and design clothing, but I have a brand I can bring to it."

Dash saw his company as appealing to more than just the inner-city crowd and he wanted the company's fashion line to reflect that. "People have a misconception about who we are," Dash told a reporter in 1999. "We like to dress down in jeans, sweatsuits, and casual shirts, as well as dress jiggy. The line will have more of a casual look because we are not trying to go all over the place with it. We're starting off with the basics and then once we establish our name, we plan to take it one step further."

It is estimated that Roc-a-Fella's clothing line pulled in $100 million in sales in 2000. The company has also branched out even further. It produced several straight-to-video films, including *Streets Is Watching*, a semiautobiographical film based on Jay-Z's song lyrics. In addition, a tour that the label helped mount in 1999, the Hard Knock Life Tour, grossed over $13.7 million, according to the company.

Now there was a downside to the rise of the hip-hop mogul. Around the time when Puff Daddy declared that it was "All About the Benjamins," hip-hop seemed to become all about the money. An insurgent street form that had been "the black CNN"—telling stories that weren't told elsewhere—started focusing, at least in the stuff that got played on the radio, on the "bling bling" and all the materialistic, capitalistic, erotic stuff—jewelry and alcohol and big-breasted women and getting paid in full.

On one level, it could be read as revolutionary. After all, the American Dream, one version of it anyway, is about acquiring wealth and status and having a home in the suburbs and two cars in the garage. But somehow, simply acquiring the bank accounts and the taste of the culture at large didn't seem like a victory. It felt like a sellout. While it was nice to see brothers partying in the Hamptons, and perhaps good to hear some rappers talking tough about hanging onto their money and building wealth, it was sad to see the political side of rap almost driven to extinction. There were a few lonely holdouts rapping about something more than material possessions: Lauryn Hill, Wyclef Jean, the Roots. But, by the end of the '90s, hip-hop was pretty much all about "the Benjamins." Listeners had to turn to underground hip-hop like Dead Prez, or to hip-hop/rock like Rage Against the Machine, if they wanted to hear rap that was real and relevant.

Still, the new wave of hip-hop moguls were brash and forceful, and they were breaking new ground for Black executives. Dash has a reputation for talking tough, for being blunt and profane, and for not being afraid to get into someone's face if he feels the situation calls for it. One magazine described him as "a belligerent E.F. Hutton." "I'm not here for everybody—I'm here for my family," Dash, who has two young children, once said. "When I first came in the business, muthafuckas was like you gotta tone your shit down and can't tell people what you think all the time. You feel my opinions. Only if one of my friends tells me I'm out of order do I take it to heart."

Dash has an impressive extended family. His cousin, Stacy Dash, is an actress; she's best known for playing Alicia Silverstone's best friend in the comedy *Clueless.* His cousin Darien is a well-known internet entrepreneur. Dash seemed to have it all—money, power, family, cool. Then, sometime around early 2001, he hooked up with Aaliyah.

The young singer was actually eight years his junior, but they shared similar tastes. They both appreciated the finer things in life, but they both enjoyed being casual as well. "She would just carry herself like such a normal individual," Dash once said. "We would pop into McDonald's or Wendy's or something, and people wouldn't believe [it]."

Soon Dash and Aaliyah were a hot item, appearing together at clubs, restaurants, record release parties, movie openings. "She was the only girl that got to hang out with my homeboys on the level of a homeboy," Dash said. "It was like being able to be with your homeboy and your girl at the same time . . . We just generally had a lot of fun together."

Suddenly, the woman who had tried to keep the

spotlight from falling on her personal life in the past was carrying on a very public affair. The pair were soon appearing in the gossip columns. *The New York Post* wrote in April of 2001: "The hottest record executive in the hip-hop world has hooked up with a simmering R&B star. Damon Dash, CEO of Roc-a-Fella Records, has been seeing Aaliyah. The two are 'inseparable,' sources said, and share a bizarre sense of humor. 'They like to go around and make scenes in hotels where Aaliyah starts screaming at Damon saying he beats her.' Dash plays along by turning on her and yelling, 'Shut up, woman!' Once they've got everybody's attention, the two of them crack up. 'They think it's fun,' a source said."

Dash and Aaliyah also made more conventional appearances in public. In May of 2001, the couple celebrated Dash's 30th birthday with a party at Grove Street Lounge in Manhattan. Aaliyah played the host and the party guests included Jay-Z, Missy Elliott, model Natane Adcock, television host Cynthia Garrett, and Mary J. Blige. A pretty good celebrity turnout by almost any standard.

Later that same month, Dash and Aaliyah were out on the town again, this time at a Mother's Day raffle in Brooklyn. At that event, rapper Jay-Z gave away several thousand dollars. Jay-Z's own mother, who attended the fundraiser, turned out to have a winning ticket but the rapper had to disqualify her.

Mothers are very big in the hip-hop world. Girlfriends are not. There's a whole catalog of hip-hop songs that rappers have written in tribute to their mothers—chief among them, Tupac's moving "Dear Mama." Love songs written specifically towards particular women, however, are more rare. When the Roots' terrific hip-hop ballad "You Got Me" (featuring Erykah Badu) was released, it stood out because it was about black-on-black love, while so many other hip-hop songs seem content to settle on black-on-black crime. When rappers talk about love, they usually mean it in a collective sense. One of Tupac's other major hits captured this theme: "I Get Around."

The hip-hop world is relentlessly, unapologetically male. There are only a few female rappers that can compete with the top male counterparts as sales forces: Lauryn Hill, Eve, and that's about it. Hip-hop is about hanging with your homies, kickin' back with your boys. P. Diddy's parties in East Hampton were essentially male fantasies. "We'll have mermaids in the pool, belly dancers and fire-eaters," Puffy once boasted to a *Daily News* reporter about an upcoming bash. "I'm gonna make personally sure that everyone has a good time." In the summer of 1999, Dash and Jay-Z rented an estate in the Hampton town of Wainscott together and held barbecues. It was all about men getting together with men and having themselves a time. Even the women in hip-hop—like Foxy Brown or Lil' Kim—often display a masculine aggressive kind of sexuality in order to fit in with the rest of the crowd. Aaliyah was cool enough to hang with Dash and his hip-hop buddies without sacrificing who she was. She had already submerged some of her personality when she was working with R.Kelly and she wouldn't do it again. When you look at photos of Dash and Aaliyah together at various functions, you can see that she had developed a certain kind of style that seems both sophisticated and street, that projects the essence of where she came from, the schooling she grew up with, and her obvious love of hip-hop.

On July 4th, 2001, Roc-a-Fella Records and Bad Boy Records held a softball game and barbecue at the Maidstone Ball Field in East Hampton, New York. P. Diddy was there, sporting a black Bad Boy uniform; he even took a turn on the pitcher's mound. Actress Tara Reid was in attendance, wearing her usual ultra-low cut jeans. Also taking part were magician David Blaine, Russell Simmons, Jay-Z (clad in a No. 6 Sixers jersey), actress Stacy Dash, and Damon Dash. Aaliyah was there as well, posing for pictures with her friend, dark-haired model Natane Adcock. That day, Aaliyah showed how comfortable she was moving between two worlds: She took a few swings with the bat (proving she could hang with the fellas) but did so while wearing a pair of very feminine, barely-there bluejean short-shorts. She also wore an almost see-through gauzy black top. She could roll with the boys, but she never let them forget that she was all woman.

Dash was smitten and had matrimony on his mind. "We were definitely gonna get married," he said. "As soon as she had time, we were getting married—like after *The Matrix.* She was the one—she was definitely the one for me. It wasn't an official proposal, we had just talked about it, you know?" Other than Will Smith and Jada Pinkett, you don't hear a whole lot about hip-hop marriages. Many fans would be surprised to know that Dr. Dre, Ice Cube, and Ice-T are all married men, despite their playa lyrics.

One of the women that Aaliyah befriended on the celebrity scene was Beyoncé Knowles of the group Destiny's Child. The two had a lot in common. Both came from close families, both had a strong sense of spirituality, and both were highly recognizable singers, in demand by talk shows and autograph seekers everywhere. Although Aaliyah was a solo act and Knowles was a member of a trio, it was no secret that in Destiny's Child, Knowles was the focal point—for fans, for cameras, for gossip pages. She was the Diana Ross of Destiny's Child, and sometimes the attention was a little hard to bear. So it was no surprise that Beyoncé and Aaliyah would hit it off as friends.

"She handled herself like a lady," Knowles told me a few weeks after Aaliyah's fatal flight. "I definitely think anyone that has that aura that she had about her has to have a great family. There was just something about her aura. You wanted to talk to her, you wanted to know her."

Because Aaliyah started out so young, she was in a fairly unique position in the music world. When young musicians cite influences, they usually name performers from other generations. Many of Aaliyah's contemporaries had actually grown up listening to Aaliyah's music. She was seen as a veteran even by artists her own age.

"Aaliyah was a big influence on all of us," said Knowles. "She was the first major young female artist to come out [in her generation]. We're about the same age, so it was very inspiring to see someone like that. She went to a performing arts high school and so did I. I just really related to her. It made me feel like, alright, if she can come out and she's young, so can I. It gave me inspiration and hope that we could do the same thing."

As a singer, Knowles was also taken with Aaliyah's singing style. Says Knowles: "Her voice was so smooth, it was so sexy and soft. She could do a lot of interesting things with her range. She could go very high and she could go very low. Her tone was just beautiful, it was sultry and sexy. But the most amazing thing is she could dance so well and sing so well, too. She just had this whole cool sexy vibe about her, the way she performed in videos and live. It even came across when she talked. But even though she was sexy she was still sweet and wholesome at the same time. There weren't too many people who were like that.

"I would have loved to have worked with her, definitely," said Knowles. "Her and Timbaland, they had a whole magic when they went into a studio and I could never wait to see what the next album was gonna be like. She always had a sound that was hot."

Aaliyah and the members of Destiny's Child first met around 1998 in Los Angeles. Aaliyah was already a star at the time and the women of Destiny's Child were just making their names. They were a bit intimidated about meeting Aaliyah. After all, she was someone they had grown up listening to. But the young star quickly put the up-and-coming trio at ease. "Aaliyah was the first celebrity to really embrace us," Knowles told me. "Everyone else was nice and they were cool but she was like extra sweet to us. And she hung out with us. She had just gotten her driver's license so she came to the hotel and picked us up and we went to the mall."

The next day, the members of Destiny's Child had a rehearsal for a video shoot, and Aaliyah and Timbaland tagged along to watch. Says Knowles:

"I'll never forget it. She came and sat through our entire rehearsal, and this is a celebrity with a platinum album. And she rewound our tape for us. I know to people that don't know celebrities that might not seem like a big thing. But I thought it was very humble of her and it says a lot about her. It was just so sweet."

Knowles and Aaliyah tried to keep in touch, but because both had demanding schedules, they rarely talked except at major events. Says Knowles: "It was hard for us to keep in touch because, you know how it is, with us doing a record and with her doing records and movies, we were always on the go. So we only really saw each other at awards shows. But I know it was always refreshing to see her and I was excited. I interviewed her two times for the MTV Movie Awards. I did the pre-show. I was really nervous about doing that because it's hard talking to celebrities sometimes. I was so happy and relieved when I got to interview her because she made me feel so comfortable, everytime."

When Knowles and Aaliyah did get a chance to talk off-camera it was usually about their punishing workload. "We used to discuss how hard it is working all the time and her schedule," says Knowles. "She told me she once flew from Australia to America for one day and then had to fly back. I just couldn't believe she flew all the way to America for one day. Now I can relate because we do things like that all the time."

I often wonder about rich folks and celebrities who continue to work absurdly long hours even long after they've already made it. Is there ever a time when a successful person can just stop and enjoy what they've done? What's the point of being rich and famous if there's never any downtime to relax and enjoy life? Of course, it's one thing when some stock trader who hates his job keeps plowing away at it even when his bank account is bursting at the seams. It's just sad to keep working at a job you hate if you don't have to. Perhaps, in the case of some artists, they simply love what they do, or are held in the grip of some artistic inspiration they can't shake. Aaliyah's drive seemed to come from love—love of success, love of music, love of pure velocity. Celebrity momentum is something that's hard to slow down once it's set in motion. At least Aaliyah, in her approximately year long relationship with Dash, had a brief moment where she seemed to give herself over to fun, to celebration, to the moment.

Weeks after Aaliyah's passing, Dash remained mostly out of the public eye. Reportedly, the grief was too difficult for him to bear. He had found the perfect woman, his soul mate, and then he had lost her. And there was no good reason for it. "She was the best person I ever knew . . . I never met a person like her in my life," said Dash. "Every day we cherished. Every memory—every day was a special event, whether it was going to a store or going to a movie or just sitting in a house. Wherever we were was like our own little party, in our own little world."

That world was about to come to an end. But not before Aaliyah made the artistic statement of her young life.

10 | the last album

Aaliyah inspired me not only to continue being an artist but to be an individual—no matter who you are or what you do, be your own person, love who you are and be proud of that.

—Alicia Keys in *Honey* magazine, November 2001

The life of a music critic sounds pretty easy. It sounds endlessly interesting, it sounds like the kind of job that makes you wonder why anyone should get paid to do it, because all it boils down to is one long vacation.

It's all true. As the music critic for *TIME,* my days aren't exactly pressured-filled. Sure, there are occasional annoyances—deadlines and deadbeat publicists, hard-to-get interviews and hard-to-write reviews. But it's not as hard as, say, covering battle in some far-off war. In my world, there are rockers and rappers, divas and jazz performers, all vying for your attention. There are concerts to attend at low-rent dives filled with patrons with piercings, and concerts at venues that are famous worldwide, such as Radio City Music Hall or Madison Square Garden. There are record release parties to make an appearance at—some held at some music executive's well-furnished apartment, others held at trendy nightspots that are hot one weekend and under new name and management the next. Then there are the interviews themselves, conducted in hotel rooms and bars, tour buses and television green rooms, artists' studios and secluded beaches.

Sometimes the subjects are unknown performers, eager to get a break, ready and willing to talk about everything and anything. Other times they are jaded superstars, reluctant to part with the tiniest bit of information. I interviewed Bob Dylan in a recording studio in New York as he was putting the finishing touches on his album *Love and Theft.* I rolled with Sean "Puff Daddy" Combs right after The Notorious B.I.G. was killed and when many people thought there might be folks gunning for him next. I interviewed Whitney Houston on a beach in Miami when she was supposed to be separated from her husband Bobby Brown, and Bobby showed up, right at the start of the interview, and the two kissed and apparently made up. I was interviewing Mariah Carey at a party once when New York Yankee Derek Jeter came by and whisked her away from me. I rapped with Lauryn Hill at her home in New Jersey until the sun went down and she didn't want to turn on the lights because she thought she could be more truthful in the dark.

You might think the names would eventually blur: Bruce Springsteen, Christina Aguilera, Shakira, Dr. Dre, Marc Anthony, Radiohead, U2, Jay-Z, Dave Matthews. But there's something about great musicians that stays with you. You have to have a kind of illuminating personality to perform up on stage and entertain 40,000 people or more all by yourself. It's hard enough for most people to keep a dinner table full of guests interested. Sometimes, when you meet entertainers offstage, it's like being caught in the high beams of a car: They're more expressive, more expansive, more ebullient than everyday folks and it can be hard to handle. Other times, when you meet performers offstage, it's almost as if a light has been switched off. It's as if they're not fully alive unless they're on stage. You still get a glow from such performers, but you have to look harder, almost squint your eyes, to catch a glimpse of what makes them great. You have to seek the greatness out, like that reporter in *Citizen Kane*, on the hunt for what made the title character so important.

Aaliyah was in that second group. She always had an air of mystery about her. She had a light, but she kept it covered. You could see the glow—

but you wanted to see more, you wanted to learn more.

I had seen her around, at awards ceremonies and hip-hop parties, but I had never gotten the chance to really sit down and talk with her. The folks handling her publicity were being very selective, very secretive, about their star and her new projects. I spent almost a year courting her and them, calling about her movies in development, asking about the status of the new album, inquiring when we could set up the interview. That's the hassle side of being a critic. In the end, pretty much every star will do an interview with a publication like *TIME* magazine. But with the top stars like Aaliyah, there is often a dance that publicists like to go through, of phone calls and lunches and off-the-record get-to-know you meetings.

Aaliyah, however, was worth the dance. There were rumors about her album that were intriguing. She was supposedly thinking of working with Trent Reznor of the hard rock band Nine Inch Nails. She was also supposedly collaborating with hip-hop/folk rocker Beck. Her new sound was said to be more mature, sexier, harder hitting. I couldn't wait to hear it.

In the summer of 2001, right before Aaliyah's album was due out, music was in a rut. Teen pop was ruling the charts: Britney Spears and 'NSync, Backstreet Boys and Mandy Moore, Jessica Simpson and 98°. Music and MTV were all about fluffy harmonies and brightly colored melodies. Many artists under 25 seemed to be playing it safe, manufacturing music, making sounds that were designed for maximum radio airplay and not designed to stand the test of time. Don't get me wrong: I love pop music, all kinds of pop music, from old Jackson 5 stuff to songs like "Say My Name" by Destiny's Child. But great pop music doesn't have to be disposable. In the summer of 2001, much of the music that was being released didn't even seem substantial enough for the recycle bin.

When I finally managed to get a copy of the new Aaliyah album, I was excited. It was a few months before the CD would be released to the general public; I had been slipped a copy early to see if I was still interested in doing an interview with her. After sitting down and listening to the album, I certainly was.

Aaliyah was the sound of a teen artist all grown up. Aaliyah still had that soft voice thing going. A conversational, almost whispering, almost prayerful voice riding on hard, hip-hop beats. But now her voice was more in her control; through training and maturity and just flat-out living she had become better able to emotionally detail a song. Her gentle voice now seemed like something elemental, a kindly wind blowing through the branches of a big tree. In her previous albums, not to take anything away from them, the sex had sometimes seemed like it was play acting. She was too young at that stage to feel everything the song was supposed to make us feel, so her light voice created a blank screen onto which we could project our own emotions. On *Aaliyah* the blank screen was filled with the colors of her own emotions. It was no wonder she titled the CD *Aaliyah.* This recording was all her.

I was invited to her record release party first. It was a small affair held at Jimmy's Uptown, an upscale restaurant in Harlem. I went with my wife. The party was in a darkened room upstairs and tracks from the new album were blaring. This kind of affair was all Aaliyah: It was very Afrocentric, a very cultural feeling, yet somehow very open and relaxed. Usually these sort of parties have a bunch of big guys hassling you for ID at the door, long lines, and so forth. This one felt like a real party, intimate and warm.

And there Aaliyah was, dressed in a flowing black dress. She looked like urban royalty. She was smiling and laughing with friends. One of her people took me up to her and we talked for a bit about nothing in particular. She was glad to be done with the album, I was looking forward to doing a sit-down with her soon, blah blah blah. I introduced her to my wife, Sharon. Aaliyah introduced me to her mother, Diane.

Many celebrities, when they are at public functions, put themselves on autopilot; they're gliding in for a landing and nobody's at the controls. There's a far-away look in their eyes, as if they're imagining other places or perhaps, in some way, they're someplace else right at that moment. That night, Aaliyah wasn't drifting. She was at that party, engaged and engaging, fully enjoying her moment.

At one point she went up on a small stage with a group of young men, most dressed in baggy forms of black clothing, and she introduced each one of them. They were all members of her production team, the folks that gave her her sound. She wanted to give them their props.

Not long afterward, I had my interview with Aaliyah. She lived in New York City—in fact she had a place on the Upper West Side, not far from where I lived—but she didn't want to meet in her apartment, she wanted to meet in a hotel. I always hate hotel interviews. There's nothing interesting you can say about a hotel room really. I mean, it's a hotel. Unless the star has trashed it in a fit of rage, a hotel room says nothing about a performer's art or mindset. But that's exactly the way Aaliyah liked it. She liked to keep the press a bit at a distance, to keep her private spaces and intimate places all to herself.

Aaliyah had some surprises in store. I was told to go to Trump Tower at One Central Park West, Suite 1214. Once there, I was instructed to ask for Veronica Lake's room. Funny that I never thought about it until later. Many superstars travel under false names to avoid fans and media besieging them with calls and requests. But Aaliyah's alias was particularly meaningful: Veronica Lake was an actress from the '40s who, like Aaliyah after her, would sweep her hair in front of her face leaving only one eye showing. It gave her a look of mystery, and of subtle glamour. There was a tragic side to the Veronica Lake story as well; months later, I wondered if Aaliyah ever knew about it. Lake had been part of the Golden Age of Hollywood, starring in such classics as *Sullivan's Travels* (1941) and *The Blue Dahlia* (1946). Her career floundered, however, and the choice parts began to elude her. She slid into alcoholism, and, at one point, worked as a bartender in a cheap hotel. She died of hepatitis at the age of 53, years before her time.

Aaliyah was waiting for me in her suite. She was wearing a loose, low-cut top, curve-hugging black jeans, black boots and modest gold jewelry. You meet a lot of beautiful people in the entertainment business and, after you've interviewed women like Naomi Campbell and Faith Hill, you come to realize that beauty isn't about beauty. I often see models and actresses and actors who appear to be attractive only under the right light or on the right day or before they open their mouths or before they start to move or make any expression of any sort on their faces. Many so-called supermodels date rather quickly, like milk on a supermarket shelf: One week they seem to be the very embodiment of loveliness, and the next week they seem too thin or too angular or too something.

True beauty doesn't come from just the outside and it doesn't come from just the inside. It really is a kind of holistic thing. And, especially with rock and roll, it comes with talent and with attitude. That's part of what's great about rap and rock: Virtually anyone, through force of will, can make themselves glamorous. Is the rapper Eve beautiful? Yes she is, because she wants to be fashionable and sexy and, because she can rap, she makes her vision of herself come true. Mick Jagger of the Rolling Stones, objectively, is a kind of strange-looking guy. But because of his attitude, because of the way he moves, because of the songs he sings and writes, he is a sex symbol to many people.

Aaliyah had a kind of grace about her. She did everything softly—she talked softly, she moved softly, she emoted softly. But she never came across as weak, just relaxed and subtle about what she wanted and where she wanted to go. There was a fetching darkness about her. Her eyes were dark, her dark hair fell past her shoulders. When she moved, there would be a sheen off her hair and it almost seemed to undulate, like the waves of a shadow-filled sea. She liked to laugh, but she did so only when something was truly funny. She had a great smile, but often all you'd get is a small tight one, as if she were reserving her full, tooth-filled smile for a happier time. When she did smile or laugh at something you said, it felt like you'd really accomplished something, like you'd gotten one through the uprights from 50 yards out or something.

So we took seats in the suite, a few inches from one another, and we began to talk. She confessed to being shy, something she's confessed to in the past, and I expressed some skepticism. Beautiful female entertainers love to say two things, I've found: 1) that they were ugly ducklings in grade school and 2) that they are really shy. I've come to believe that they say 1) so other not-so-attractive women don't hate them for being beautiful and that they say 2) to flirt with male interviewers. Guys are always intrigued by the prospect of bringing a hot-looking woman out of her shell.

But how can an entertainer really be shy? I asked. After all, she had danced in sexy costumes on stage, sung about sexual subjects and, in her new film *Queen of the Damned,* she even had a love scene. How shy could she be?

Aaliyah admitted that she had two sides, and the public one was more outgoing. "When I get in front of the camera or when I get on stage I transform into another person," she told me. "It's that moment before getting on stage or in front of the camera that's the most difficult for me. Once I'm out there, it's all good."

So what about that love scene? Self-confessed shy girl Aaliyah wasn't at all shy about talking about that. In fact, she warmed to the subject and seemed to really enjoy talking about her character in *The Queen of the Damned.* "Akasha is very manipulative," she said. "She and Lestat get into a tub, and I seduce him. So I had to kiss him on the chest and draw blood." Then she added: "I was very shy about it." Hey, once you've sucked blood out of another actor's chest with the cameras rolling, it's too late to go back to shy.

Aaliyah went on: "It's a very important role. What I like about it is she's not throughout the whole film. She comes in near the middle. She's anticipated for a while throughout the film. She's very powerful, very evil. And spoiled. She always got her way and she's a bit of a brat. So there's a lot I had to bring out of myself and find within me and bring to the forefront in order to bring her to life."

It was then that we began to discuss the other major project in her future: the sequel to one of the greatest films ever made, *The Matrix.* Now, in my opinion, there are only two kinds of art, and only two kinds of artists: originals and imitators. Originals are breakthroughs, they set new standards, take us to new places, open our minds to experiences we had never quite imagined or, if we had, that we never believed would be brought into being. Originals often draw on the past, but, in doing so, they create something wholly new that is copied and drawn upon for generations afterwards. Bob Marley and the Wailers' album *Catch a Fire* is an original: It wasn't the first reggae album, but it established the form for all time. Francis Ford Coppola's *The Godfather* is an original: it turned the gangster movie into high art and set the table for all the films and TV programs that would follow it, from *New Jack City* to HBO's *The Sopranos.* J.R.R. Tolkien's *The Lord of the Rings* is an original: Almost every work of fantasy that followed it owed it some debt. Aretha Franklin, Prince, Bob Dylan, J.D. Salinger, Thomas Pynchon and the poet Derek Walcott, and the first two *Star Wars* movies are originals. Elvis, Limp Bizkit, and the third and fourth movies in the *Star Wars* series are all works of imitation.

The Matrix is an original work. It tells the story of a computer programmer named Thomas A. Anderson (played by Keanu Reeves) who comes to discover that the world is a computer-generated illusion and that machines are actually ruling the world. With the help of two revolutionaries, Morpheus (played by Laurence Fishburne) and Trinity (Carrie-Anne Moss), he discovers his inner powers and leads the fight against the evil world-ruling computers. The movie was directed by Andy and Larry

Wachowski (a brother filmmaking team) and the action scenes in the movie were staged by the great Yuen Wo-Ping, whose work is legendary in Hong Kong. The special effects and fight scenes in the movie—especially the moments in which time seems to slow down as the actors kick and punch and twirl through the air in slo-mo combat—have been copied by innumerable other movies, videos, and even commercials.

Aaliyah was impressed with the original *Matrix* even before it became a big hit. Said Aaliyah: "When I saw it I thought—'What I wouldn't have given to be Trinity.' There's nothing like a strong woman who kicks butt. When I heard they were doing a sequel, I was like 'I want to be in *The Matrix!* I want to be in *The Matrix!*' It's like the *Star Wars* of our time."

When I talked to Aaliyah, she knew very little about her part. Pretty much all she knew was that her character was going to be called "Zee" and that there was a good chance she was going to have some fight scenes. She was very excited about the role. *The Matrix* was more than a movie, it was a cultural phenomenon—her presence in the series (she was signed to do the next two installments) would have helped to broaden her fame and to make her a household name. It also would have linked her forever with a work of popular art that had real impact and influence. Such associations are priceless.

Certain actors transcend them: Harrison Ford may have played Han Solo in *Star Wars* but he is remembered for much more. But, in the end, once you're in a work of art of true originality, it almost doesn't matter. Forever afterwards, you'll be part of remembrances and retrospectives, anniversary celebrations and remakes. So what if Mark Hamill never really made a great movie besides the first two installments of *Star Wars?* He's going to live forever on video, DVD, and whatever other formats they come up with. Aaliyah, by being cast in *The Matrix* series, had positioned herself for her own cinematic immortality.

Still, music was her first love, as she put it, and even as she made her movies, she was working to bring her new album into being. While she was in Melbourne filming *The Queen of the Damned,* she essentially worked two shifts, making the movie at night and recording her album by day. "I tried my best that when I was doing one thing I wasn't doing the other," she told me. "I was truly able to separate the two."

She was proud of the results. She loved all the songs on the album, but there were a few that were closer to her heart than others. "Some of my babies are 'Never No More' and 'More Than a Woman,' " she said. I could see why those songs stood out to her; both tracks were demonstrations of her coming into her own as a singer and an artist. "Never No More" is a song about a defiant woman who decides to break out of a relationship that is becoming physically abusive. "'Never No More' is one of my favorites because of the subject matter," Aaliyah said. "I'm proud of that song. I'm hoping a lot of women feel it."

"More Than a Woman" is another standout number from the album; it's a sexy, voluptuous track and there's no doubt that the vocalist singing it has moved from girl to full-bodied woman. The subject matter of the song is a woman begging her lover to choose her over all others, but, because of the inner strength of the vocals and the power of the song's rhythms, the track becomes a kind of declaration of independence. "The track is absolutely phenomenal," said Aaliyah. "It's very club, very upbeat." You get the feeling, after listening to "More Than a Woman," that the woman in question will be just fine on her own, thank you, and that whatever man is considering passing on her charms is making a tragic mistake.

Who in their right mind would leave a woman like Aaliyah? Her image in her new videos also captured her new maturity, her willingness to flash her kinkier, stranger side. In the video for "We Need a Resolution," a track that features a rap by Timbaland, Aaliyah appears with a large snake entwined around her. In other scenes, she is slightly smeared with mud. She seems to be saying that even with a bit of dirt on her, even with a symbol of temptation wrapped around her, she can maintain an aura of innocence, intelligence, and sexiness. Says Aaliyah: "There's a dark side of me that comes out in everything I do."

Aaliyah's image isn't one created for her by others. But she is someone who is more than willing to admit that she actively seeks out the advice of her friends and family, and very often goes with it. "I definitely go with the advice of others," she said. "With my team. It's a collaborative effort with everything that I do. I ask my manager, I ask my brother, I ask Static [one of her key producers and songwriters], the people at my record company. The final decision is mine."

She went on: "It's definitely a family affair. I really wouldn't have it any other way. There's a comfort there because there are people that love me and I know they have my best interests at heart no matter what. But the final decision is mine. So they protect me, they watch out for me, but they let me be free at the same time. And we're pretty good about separating family and business."

Aaliyah was also pretty resolute about separating public and private. She dodged questions about her alleged marriage to her former producer R.Kelly. When I asked her if she was still in touch with R.Kelly, she gave me a firm, frosty "No." When I asked if she would ever work with him again, she repeated the answer and the tone. Still, her private life wasn't completely off limits to scrutiny. It seemed to me, as in her new video, that she liked to hint at private quirkiness, liked to suggest that she had some wild things going on behind her closed doors. She told me her apartment in Manhattan was littered with Egyptian objects: cat statues, Egyptian pictures, even a dresser shaped like a pyramid. "I have a bit of an obsession with Egypt," she said.

Despite her interest in history, her main focus was on her own future. Child stars usually don't turn out well; they often end up fading into obscurity, checking into rehab centers, sadly and desperately trying to reclaim the glory moments they had experienced before they could even understand, appreciate and enjoy their significance. I asked Aaliyah if she felt, if by becoming a star so young, she had missed out on having a real childhood. "I'm 22, I've been in this since 15. I'm basically a veteran and yet I still have many places to go. I'm still young. I have no regrets. My parents made sure that I was involved in not just the show side of it, but the business side. I know about my contracts, I know about every little detail as far as the business is involved. So one day I can sit back and seriously enjoy the fruits of my labor."

Those words echoed in my mind a few weeks later.

11 | more than a woman

With every breath like it's the last.
With every blink like a freeze-frame of a precious moment.
With every touch to record how we once were human.
We are destined to be something more.
Aaliyah, you have fulfilled that destiny.

—RASHAD HAUGHTON, AALIYAH'S BROTHER

What would you do if you knew today was the last day of your life? How would you act differently? Of course, most people never know when, and if, the end is approaching. Terrorists bent on destroying themselves and others can plan their own doom, but even they don't know what the outcome of their schemes will be. Suicide victims, people with terminal illnesses, the elderly, and the infirm sometimes anticipate their own demise. But for most people—and certainly for Aaliyah—the last day of one's life looks like any other day.

And Aaliyah's last day, Saturday, August 25, 2001, seemed like a beautiful one. She had just wrapped up filming what would be her final video, for the song "Rock the Boat." It has an upbeat dance beat, with a come-on chorus. The director, Hype Williams, would later tell MTV News that Aaliyah and the crew spent the whole day shooting. He was very proud of the final result. "It's a special project," said Williams. "Everybody put their heart and soul into the work, as we always do, with the intent that the world would enjoy it. I know there's a lot of pain involved, but that's all the more reason people would appreciate what we've done as a group."

In my opinion, there was probably a little trouble in paradise. The few times I had spoken with Aaliyah, I had seen how much pressure she was under. She was being pulled in a million different directions. Her schedule was incredibly booked. I usually don't feel sorry for overbooked stars—hey, it's their call if they want to get on the treadmill of fame—but in Aaliyah's case I really wondered about the strain she was feeling. I asked her about her demanding schedule and she gave me one of her rare smiles, and indicated that she had picked this life and accepted the pressures as a necessary part of being a superstar.

Still, looking back on her last day on Abaco Island, I can't help but wonder what role her schedule played in her choices. Her album *Aaliyah* was indeed a hit, but perhaps not as big a hit as people might have expected. It had debuted on the

Billboard charts at number two, one step below the reigning champ, Alicia Keys, a hip-hop soul newcomer who, at the age of 20, was even younger than Aaliyah. It must have been galling for Aaliyah and her team to finish second to the new kid on the block. After all, she was once the new kid on the block. Now, at age 22, Aaliyah was fighting to maintain her superstar status, battling to establish herself as an adult artist.

The first single off Aaliyah's album, "We Need a Resolution," was a fine, moving performance, but radio hadn't jumped on it. Surprisingly, it never even made it into the Top 40, peaking at 59 on the charts. No doubt, Aaliyah's record company needed to get another single off the album onto the charts, preferably with a higher placement, to help drive sales of the album. Aaliyah, I was told by a member of her publicity team, was a major priority for Virgin Records, a major label that worked with Blackground to put out Aaliyah's CDs. A lot of people had a lot riding on her success.

If Aaliyah had known that August 25, 2001 was going to be the last day of her life, would she have made different choices? If she hadn't been such a driven businesswoman, if she hadn't taken such pride in the success of her career, would she have made the same moves? She had appointments to keep back in the States. She had the MTV Video

Music Awards to prepare for and she had a movie, the sequel to *The Matrix*, to get ready for, and a few more vocal overdubs to do for *The Queen of the Damned*. With all that waiting for her, she had every reason to want to get back home in a hurry.

"God that girl could have gone so far," Michael Rymer, director of *The Queen of the Damned*, told me later. "She had such clarity about what she wanted. Nothing was gonna step in her way. No ego, no nervousness, no manipulation. There was nothing to stop her.

"That's why, when she died, I was so shocked, because she had me convinced of her trajectory. Not by telling me she was gonna be this or that, but because of who she was, that she was on her way to something special. And she had such a clear vision of where she was. There was a moment after she died where—and you mourn these things in strange ways—but I remember getting a little upset and saying to myself, 'I trusted you, you more or less told me you had places to go and this wasn't where you were thinking of going.' "

Aaliyah left to catch an airplane out of the Bahamas sometime after 5 P.M. A taxi was called to take her to Marsh Harbour airport. Aaliyah's final moments seemed to be happy ones. She started singing as soon as she entered the cab and continued singing all the way to the airport.

According to one report in *The New York Post*, Aaliyah was stopped by a young fan at the airport who wanted a picture as a souvenir. Aaliyah, passport in hand, hurrying to make it back home, did what she usually did: She cheerfully agreed. "She seemed happy, but told me 'I'm exhausted, all this running around is wearing me down,' " said Alvin Lightdouin, the 17-year-old fan who posed with the singer. The two chatted for 15 minutes and Aaliyah gave him a hug. Lightdouin praised her for recently giving $20,000 to charity. She told him, "God blessed me with money and now it's time to give back." Then she was off.

At some point after 6 P.M., Aaliyah boarded a waiting plane—a twin-engine Cessna 402B. Besides Aaliyah, there were eight other passengers on board: Luis Morales III, 30, the pilot; assistant hairstylist Anthony Dodd, 34, of Los Angeles; hairstylist Eric Foreman, 29, of Hollywood; Aaliyah's bodyguard Scott Gallin, 41, of Pompano Beach, Florida; Keith Wallace, 49, of Los Angeles (a close friend of Aaliyah's mother who had been serving as a surrogate parent on the trip); Blackground executive Gina Smith, 30, of New Jersey; Douglas Kratz, 28, of Hollywood (director of video production for Virgin Records America); and makeup artist Christopher Maldonado, 32, of New York. The plane crashed shortly after takeoff, killing all on board, including Aaliyah. Gallin survived the initial impact and spent his last few moments worrying about his famous client. Ambulance drivers reportedly said that the hulking bodyguard kept asking about Aaliyah's condition. He died soon afterwards.

In early October, I talked to Claude Sawyer, 25, a charter pilot who witnessed the crash. He was working on some machinery about half a mile away when he saw the Cessna go down. "I saw the plane go up and then it banked to the left and nosed in," he told me. He said the plane was only "60 to 100 feet" off of the ground when it began its fatal dive.

Sawyer, who was born in the Bahamas, also works as a fireman, and so when he saw the accident, he quickly took action. "I went to get a firetruck," he said. "Two other firemen were in the area and they also went to the site of the crash." When Sawyer arrived at the scene he was stunned by what he saw. "I've seen crashes before, but that was probably one of the worst ones," he said. "It was pretty devastating. The aircraft was broken into pieces and some of the seats were ejected from the aircraft."

Sawyer tried to help, but found he was already too late. Said Sawyer: "We were hoping we could save some people. Before our arrival, the fireman who was there advised us that there were people from the crash who were still living at the time." The crash occurred in swampy ground and there was fire in spots surrounding the site and some of the bodies of the victims were also on fire. At that point, three people had survived the crash, but when Sawyer saw them, they appeared to be mortally wounded. The survivors were all men; Aaliyah had already been killed. In the end, even the trio of passengers who survived the initial impact eventually succumbed to their injuries: One died enroute to Princess Margaret Hospital in Nassau, another arrived at the same hospital in a coma and died at 3:28 A.M. on Sunday, and the third died at the Marsh Harbour Clinic. Says Sawyer: "It was amazing that they survived as long as they did from what I saw."

Sawyer says he won't speculate on what went wrong with the aircraft: "From what I saw there were a number of things that could have gone wrong. We left it up to the investigators to determine the cause."

After the crash, a controversy raged in the media about the possibility that the small plane was overloaded. Leeland Russell of the Abaco Police Department told VH1's "Behind the Music" that "Some persons were saying that the pilot [was] arguing with the passengers saying that it was too much weight to put on the plane. But the passengers, I understand, said that 'their luggage must go and we must go. [We] cannot leave anything.' " After the accident, according to a spokesperson for the National Transportation Safety Board, representatives from the NTSB, the Federal Aviation Administration, Cessna, and the manufacturer of the plane's engines went to Abaco on a fact-finding trip. The NTSB issued this brief report:

> On August 25, 2001, about 18:45 eastern daylight time, a Cessna 402B, N8097W, registered to Skystream Inc. and operated by Blackhawk International Airways Inc, as a 14 CFR Part 135 on-demand charter flight, crashed shortly after takeoff from runway 27 at Marsh Harbor Airport, Bahamas. Visual meterological conditions prevailed at the time. A VFR flight plan was filed, but not activated. The airplane was destroyed, the commercial-rated pilot and eight passengers were fatally injured. The flight was originated at the time of the accident and was destined to Opa-Locka, Florida.
>
> The airplane was seen lifting off the runway, and then nose down, impacting in a marsh on the south side of the departure end of runway 27. The baggage from the airplane was removed and weighed. The total weight of the luggage, fuel on board at the time of the accident, plus the weight of the passengers showed that the total gross weight of the airplane was substantially exceeded. Preliminary center of gravity calculations showed that the center of

> gravity was significantly outside the flight envelope past the aft center of gravity.
>
> Preliminary information indicated that the pilot was not approved to act as pilot-in-command in the accident aircraft under 14 CFR Part 135. The owner of Blackhawk International Airways Inc. Mr. Gilbert Chacon, has only communicated to investigators through his attorney, and has not produced the aircraft or engine logbooks. The complete maintenance history of the airplane is unknown.
>
> The engines and airframe were torn down and examined at Marsh Harbour; no discrepancies were found. The propellers will be shipped to Miami, Florida, for examination at a later date.

Because the Aaliyah accident took place in the Bahamas, officials from that country, not the American authorities, are heading up the investigation. The chief inspector on the case, Randy Butler of Bahamas' Civil Aviation Department, told me on October 5, 2001, that "The investigation at this time is continuing. We have not completed it as yet."

A report carried in August of 2001 by the Associated Press, *The Palm Beach Post*, and other news outlets alleged that Luis Morales, the pilot of the plane, had been sentenced to probation on

August 13, 2001 for being found with a small amount of cocaine in his car during a traffic stop in Pompano Beach, Florida. There were additional reports, including one in the *New York Times* on September 8, 2001 and another in the *Sun-Sentinel* (Fort Lauderdale), that questioned whether Morales was qualified to fly the plane.

Gabriel Penagaricano, a San Juan, Puerto Rico-based lawyer who is serving as a spokesperson for the family of Luis Morales, told me in an interview on October 4, 2001, that questions about Morales' flight record are "the words of a fool." Says Penagaricano: "[Morales] was a young man, totally dedicated to his profession and had set his sights on flying for one of the major airlines. In the meantime, he was doing what everyone else of his age and experience does, which is to fly for a charter operator in order to build up flying time." Penagaricano says Morales was "certainly" qualified to fly a Cessna 402B. He also says the fact that Morales had a criminal record had "nothing to do" with the crash. Penagaricano told me it would only be relevant "if was he was under the influence of some sort of controlled substance at the time he was performing as a pilot which is not the case in this matter."

Penagaricano did express concern that a Bahamian agency, and not an American agency like the NTSB, was taking the lead on the case. "They certainly do not have the technical expertise, nor do they have the laboratory resources that the NTSB has," says Penagaricano. "And I believe that is a fact recognized throughout the world." Penagaricano said the case was a complex one that required an agency with the means to investigate it fully. Said Penagaricano: "The expertise of the NTSB is unquestioned. And I for one would feel a lot more comfortable if the Bahamian government had turned the investigation over to the NTSB because it is the NTSB who could have told us to a very high degree of certainty what it was that happened. They could have certainly discarded any doubt that everyone will have as to whether those engines were in fact functioning properly or whether they were a contributing factor to the accident."

Butler, however, says that Bahamian officials can indeed handle the investigation, and that they will keep American investigators informed. "The investigation is being controlled and handled by the Civil Aviation Department, by the Bahamas," says Butler. "The U.S. are parties to it, and they are parties because it's a U.S. registered airplane, U.S. certificate pilot, U.S. company that was operating the aircraft, U.S. citizens."

Meanwhile, images of the accident have been printed and broadcast around the world. Some still pictures, as well as moving video, from the crash site have even made their way onto file-sharing services such as Morpheus. The pictures are pretty ugly: twisted metal and flame-licked debris. It's hard not to wonder what went through the minds of the passengers in those final moments, or whether they had time to think at all. After the World Trade Center attacks on September 11th, there were reports of victims calling loved ones from the hijacked planes, and from the burning towers, telling their significant others that they were done for, and delivering their final good-byes via cell-phone, or on messages left on voice mail. But most people don't have that chance. It all ends unexpectedly and horribly and we never know what the people we care about will take away from the tragedy. We never get a chance to choose our final impression.

Said Rashad in October 2001: "It really boggles everyone [that] from Day One, every single video she ever shot there's always been myself or my mother or father there. The circumstances surrounding this last video were really strange because my mother had eye surgery and she couldn't fly. That really bothered her because she always traveled. My dad had to take care of my mom at that time. And I went to a trip to Australia to visit some friends. We really couldn't understand why we weren't there. You ask yourself maybe we could have stopped it. But you can't really answer that question. There's always gonna be that question of why."

Perhaps that's all the more reason to live an examined life, a lived life, a life with no regrets. Maybe Aaliyah was onto something, maybe that's why she packed her 22 years with two movies and three albums and millions of records sold. She didn't have to worry about how she'd leave us. She knew she had already left us with plenty. "It was a tremendous change and a tremendous improvement from that first album to that third album," Wendelin Peddy, Aaliyah's vocal coach, told me. "There's no telling where she may have gone had she still been with us. The style she had was her own. Now others that come behind her will probably imitate her."

The week after Aaliyah's death, sales of her final album increased from 62,000 copies to 305,000 copies and the album jumped from number 19 on the Billboard charts all the way to number 1. The move pushed her album ahead of Mary J. Blige, ahead of Alicia Keys, ahead of 'NSync, and Jennifer Lopez. The sales, of course, didn't really matter. But finally, after her death, the whole pop world was catching on to what a fine album *Aaliyah* really was.

What would you do differently if you knew today was the last day of your life? How would your choices change if you knew the end was near?

Aaliyah once told *Honey* magazine, "I feel like I'm really just getting started. I don't know what's going to happen in the next five or ten years. At some point I want to have a family and settle down, but I don't see that happening for a very long time because I really love this. This is my life, my world."

Not long after Aaliyah's death, Beyoncé Knowles of Destiny's Child told me about the night she heard of Aaliyah's passing: "I was in Indianapolis. We were on our way to Chicago. It happened while we were onstage actually. We got off stage and somebody paged our assistant. We thought it was a rumor. Then someone else called, and somebody else. I was hoping and praying it wasn't true. But I just started crying."

"Everyone else was like, 'Beyoncé it might be a rumor.' But I just had a feeling. We turned on the news and nothing was on at first and finally, on one station, they reported it happened. The whole tour bus, we were all in tears. We were all praying now. Immediately I called my mom and we prayed together on the phone. Then I called my dad. It was very sad. I couldn't sleep the next day or the next. None of us could. Then one day I realized she was an angel. I think we should be grateful that she blessed us for the 22 years she was on the earth and now she's with God.

"To this day, every night I pray for her family and I pray for her. I know she is with God now. I'm not worried about her, she is in a better place. Her relationship with her mother is like my relationship with my mom. So I can only imagine how her family must feel. I just pray for them."

She continued: "I think all of us have to just take a second and reflect on our lives and what is really important to us. We have to realize this is a job, yes, but we still have to live our lives. Because you never know when your time is here. It made all of us say we need to slow down, and we need to be more cautious, and we need to not get on those small planes."

She went on: "My whole perspective on life is different now. It made me call people that I hadn't talked to just to tell them I love them. Aaliyah mended a lot of relationships that way; she changed a lot of people's perspective on life and work."

As it turns out, Aaliyah may not have been been leaving the Bahamas because of work, but because of love. Annie Russell, the local driver who headed the crew of taxis working with the video crew, told me that she thinks, based on a conversation Russell had with Gina Smith, the Blackground executive travelling with Aaliyah, that the young singer left the island to get back to Damon Dash. "[Aaliyah] wanted to go," Russell told me. "Nobody told her to go. Gina who was with her said she missed her boyfriend."

Not long before the crash, Aaliyah told the

German newspaper *Die Zeit* about a recurring dream she was having in which she was flying away from her troubles. "It is dark in my favorite dream," Aaliyah said. "Someone is following me. I don't know why. I'm scared. Then suddenly, I lift off. Far away. How do I feel? As if I am swimming in the air. Weightless. Nobody can reach me. Nobody can touch me. It's a wonderful feeling." Perhaps on that last day, on that last flight, Aaliyah was feeling that same sense of euphoric escape.

Here's the way I'd like to remember Aaliyah: singing in that taxi on her way to the airport. Evening would have been coming on, and the night was warm, and there she was, singing. It tells me that whatever she was thinking, whatever pressures she was under, whatever she was feeling about her sales or her schedule or her love life, she was essentially happy. Many superstar singers don't sing unless they have to, they don't use their golden pipes unless there's money on the table. Aaliyah was singing for no reason other than she loved to sing. That was her world, no matter how many other possible worlds there were out there. Despite everything, or maybe because of everything, she still loved to sing.

epilogue

I'm still young. I have no regrets.

—AALIYAH, IN HER LAST INTERVIEW WITH ME

After the tragedy came the tributes.

The gangsta rapper DMX, who had appeared with Aaliyah in *Romeo Must Die* and performed with her on the soundtrack, said this in an open letter to his former co-star: "Dearest Sweet Aaliyah: We didn't know each other long, or see each other much, but we became instant and sincere friends. I have trouble accepting the fact that you are gone—so I won't. It'll be like we went without seeing each other for a while. I thank you for the movie opportunities and for the chance to work with you. But I can see why God wanted you closer to him because you truly were an angel on earth. See you soon, and in my one special way—I Love You! You'll always be with us!! Blessed Journey!"

Aaliyah's "Auntie Gladys," Gladys Knight, said this: "Her star had just begun to shine so brightly. Though she was ours only for a short time, what a time it was. I love you Aaliyah, and I will miss her for the rest of my life."

Damon Dash, Aaliyah's boyfriend, had this to say: "I am crushed and heartbroken over the loss of such a beautiful and talented woman whom I loved deeply and who meant the world to me. Words can't decribe how much I will miss her. She was my best friend and will remain in my heart forever. My thoughts and prayers go out to Aaliyah's family and everyone affected by this tragedy."

The intense expressions of grief caught a lot of media by surprise. Who was this young woman?, some pundits wondered. Why do so many people care so much? Some fans were calling her "hip-hop's Lady Di." Posters promoting her album *Aaliyah* that had been up in major cities, such as New York and Los Angeles, became makeshift memorials as passersby scrawled out their feelings and signed their names. Message boards on the internet filled up with outpourings of sorrow. It was like Tupac, but not quite. It was like Kurt, but not really. Some of the other musicians who had died in the recent past had been somewhat self-destructive. When their deaths were announced there was sadness, there was surprise, but perhaps not shock. Tupac had forecast his early death, he had almost bragged about it. He had rapped about the dangerous angry world he traveled in, and so when it enveloped him, his followers mourned, but understood. Kurt Cobain's music was full of jagged edges and references to guns and grief, his lyrics swirled with inner turmoil and inner pain. His death was a blow, but afterwards, it seemed as if one could at least trace his suicide's roots.

With Aaliyah it was different. No one saw it coming. It wasn't part of her lifestyle or her music. So we mourned Kurt, we mourned Tupac, and now we mourned Aaliyah.

And there was more mourning to come.

When I attended the 2001 MTV Video Music Awards on September 6, Aaliyah's spirit seemed to hang heavily over the proceedings. There were other big things happening in music: Michael Jackson was readying a comeback album entitled *Invincible*, Britney Spears had a new song due out called "I'm a Slave 4 U," and Mariah Carey had suffered a very public emotional breakdown right before the release of her first major Hollywood movie. Big things. But next to the death of Aaliyah, it all seemed small.

Awards shows are typically boring affairs. I've

been to most of the major ones: the Grammys, the Emmys, and so on. If you're watching on television they seem exciting and fabulous and full of fun. In truth, most awards shows are designed for television, so there are a lot of dead spots where the commercials are slipped in. The viewers at home see the ads. The people in the audience just sit there listening to silence. The funny little short films you see on awards shows are often not visible to the people in the audience. Again, there's mostly just a whole lot of silence. As a result, awards shows are typically big empty circuses that go on for hours and are only worth going to if you're the kind of person who relishes telling everyone at your office or dorm room how you were at that awards show they watched on television last night.

After Aaliyah's death, however, the MTV Video Music Awards were a bit different. It was like that scene in *How the Grinch Stole Christmas* where the Grinch's heart grows a few sizes. This year, the awards seemed to have a heart, to have a purpose, no matter what was going on around it.

The Video Music Awards had their usual star-studdedness. They were held at New York City's Metropolitan Opera House, an incongruous venue that was supposed to bring out, by contrast, the anarchic spirit of the participants. But it all seemed tame. On my way in, I spied Busta Rhymes going past the ticket-takers with a four-member posse in tow (somehow I imagined Busta with a much bigger posse). A few moments later I nearly ran into Jon Bon Jovi in the hallway wearing a big cowboy hat (he's bigger than you might expect, but then again that might have just been the hat).

I felt like the entertainment world was mourning two deaths that night: the passing of Aaliyah and the sad demise of pop music itself. The performers that night ranged all the way from atrocious to inspiring. Britney Spears performed with a snake—something Aaliyah had already done in her video "We Need a Resolution," and in a much more alluring fashion besides. 'NSync did an exhausted rendition of their song "Pop," before Michael Jackson appeared and stole the show away from them.

There were a few bright spots. That's why you watch awards shows: for the moments. They may be few and far between, but one good performance, one outrageous action, can justify the whole night. And this night had a few performances worth remembering. Up-and-coming soul diva Alicia Keys, the act that had kept Aaliyah away from the top spot on the charts, gave a solid performance, holding it down for young singer-songwriters of real talent. The rock band U2 delivered a fine performance as well, reminding all the viewers that there was still real rock and roll out there. And the video that was the big winner of the night, Fatboy Slim's "Weapon of Choice," was a quirky reminder of the entertainment power of a smart video. Directed by Spike Jonze, it features character actor Christopher Walken dancing around an empty hotel lobby to Fatboy Slim's clubland beats—it's simple, direct, and incredibly cool. Doug Kratz, the Virgin Records rep who died in the crash with Aaliyah, had worked on the video.

The highlight of the evening—or perhaps I should say the most emotional moment of the evening—came during the tribute to Aaliyah. Missy "Misdemeanor" Elliott, singer Ginuwine, and Timbaland joined Aaliyah's brother, Rashad, on stage for a tribute. There was no singing, no rapping, no dancing. Just some emotional, straight-from-the heart testimonials about what Aaliyah meant to them, and to pop music. Earlier, in a phone call to Total Request Live, Timbaland said, "She was like blood, and I lost blood. Me and her together had this chemistry. I kinda lost half of my creativity to her." That night, on stage, Missy Elliott said, "I think what we've got to learn out of this is to appreciate each other while we're here on earth. I love you, Aaliyah, and you're forever missed." Elliot was wearing a white jacket with a portrait of Aaliyah on the back and the fallen singer's name on the side.

Then Rashad read a short poem about his sister.

You couldn't see it on television, but there was a moment there: After the camera cut to footage of Aaliyah, Rashad paused in front of a huge television screen projecting an image of his sister. Her face on the screen was taller than he was, and from where I was, sitting in the balcony, he seemed swallowed up in it. When he paused, it seemed as if he didn't want to leave the stage—it was almost as if he realized every act he took to lay his sister to rest put her further and further away from him. To stop mourning is to decide that one stage of one's life is over. So Rashad paused in front of his sister's face. And then he walked off stage.

"I have to honestly say that everything is worth it," Aaliyah said on the MTV videotape. "The hard work, the times when you're tired, the times when you're a bit sad, the good moments when you're on stage performing in front of thousands of people. In the end, it's all worth it because it really makes me happy and I wouldn't trade it for anything else in the world, I honestly wouldn't. There's nothing better than loving what you do. I've got good friends, I've got a beautiful family, and I've got a career, a career that's blossoming and still growing and I am truly blessed and I thank God for his blessings every single chance that I get."

Rashad said later: "What I remember the most about her? Well, first in that video ["Rock the Boat"] the scene that sticks out the most is the very last scene where she's under the water. She always had a really big fear of water—the ocean. In the video actually she couldn't use the breath regulator. But what I remember most about her is she was a perfectionist, she was fearless and she was a role model for every young girl to follow their dreams and never let anyone give you any limitations. She actually held her breath for that scene, because she knew she had to get that scene, she knew how beautiful it was going to be. In that scene if you look at it she looks like an angel and she's floating. And that's how we all should remember her—as an angel."

Weeks later, I talked to Timbaland about Aaliyah and the emotion was still with him. His voice was heavy and halting with loss. I could tell that he didn't really want to talk but there was something inside compelling him to speak; he had to get his feelings out, he wanted to tell the world how much Aaliyah meant to him. Aaliyah had helped make Timbaland, and he had helped to make her. Artistic collaborations that work are rarer than true love, rarer than good marriages. Think of the Police: After Sting left the group no member of the trio, including Sting, ever found a partnership as fruitful.

So Timbaland still seemed a bit in shock. He found it difficult to sum up Aaliyah's life, except to say, "What comes in my head? Just special. Very unique. That's what comes to my mind. That's what she was."

Aaliyah's funeral, held on August 31, 2001 in New York City, was special as well. It was a storybook ceremony for a woman whose life, though charmed, hadn't had a storybook ending. Somber fans, the night before the actual event, began to gather outside of St. Ignatius Loyola Roman Catholic Church, where the services were to be held. Some were in tears, many clutched copies of her albums or pictures of her. A few, to pass the time, sang Aaliyah's best-known hits. The next morning, the singer's body, held in a glass paneled hearse, was pulled through the streets of Manhattan by a white carriage led by two cream-colored horses. The hearse was ornamented with dozens of roses, including many pink ones, as that was her favorite color. The carriage didn't have to go far. It went from the Frank E. Campbell Funeral Home on the Upper East Side to the services at St. Ignatius on Park Avenue. Aaliyah's parents, Diane and Michael Haughton, and her brother, Rashad, walked behind the hearse, now and again holding tight to each other, trying to find some solace in family. Finally, they entered the church.

The private Catholic funeral mass was attended by a glittering throng of musical celebrities, including Jay-Z, Sean "P. Diddy" Combs, Lil' Kim, Missy

Elliott, Mya, Gladys Knight, Busta Rhymes, and Usher. The celebrity guests—including boxer Mike Tyson and Busta Rhymes—sat in a special section reserved for luminaries. Gladys Knight and Jet Li were also in attendance and sat nearby.

Ten pallbearers pulled the 800-pound silver-plated coffin into the church where it was set down next to two large pictures. One was of the singer, in all her beauty, and the other was of her grandmother, Mintis Hankerson, whom Aaliyah was especially close to before she died of breast cancer. A quote from Aaliyah was on the grandmother's photo: "You are the sun that inspired me and the moon that got me through my nights—love, Aaliyah."

Aaliyah told an interviewer from *FHM* magazine in August 2000 about a very special tattoo that she had. "I have three tattoos. I have my initial and a star on my hand—my four friends have the same star on their wrists, too," she said. "I have a music symbol and a dove on my back—which I wanted to get in honor of my grandmother who passed away two years ago. That one was the most painful. I was straddling a chair, sweating up a storm, but kept saying through gritted teeth: 'This is for my grandmother.' "

At Aaliyah's service, Rashad delivered a 15-minute eulogy that was graceful and emotional. He said: "Aaliyah, you left, but I'll see you always next to me and I can see you smiling through the sunshine.

When our life is over, our book is done. I hope God keeps me strong until I see her again." He then read the names of the other eight crash victims and asked all those in attendance to remember them in their prayers.

Then came the music.

The church choir sang "Ave Maria." It had been Aaliyah's high school audition song. Now it was her exit music.

Ave Maria
Mater Dei
Ora pro nobis peccatoribus
Ora pro nobis
Ora, ora pro nobis peccatoribus
Nunc et in hora mortis
Et in hora mortis nostrae
Et in hora mortis nostrae
Et in hora mortis nostrae
Ave Maria

The hour-long ceremony was then over. But there was one more song to be sung. As the coffin was carried out of the church, Diane walked alongside of it. She seemed to not want to let her daughter go. They had been through so much together, they had gone so far together. Diane was her daughter's business partner, she was her daughter's closest confidante, and she was her daughter's constant traveling companion—except on two trips: the one from Abaco Island, and the trip her daughter was now about to take. Diane placed her left hand on her daughter's coffin and kept it there all the way up to the church doors.

Then she began singing "One in a Million." Some of the other mourners joined in.

After the private event, fans stood by reverently and watched while Aaliyah's casket was loaded into a waiting hearse. Then, like something out of a fairy tale, twenty-two white doves were released into the air, one for every year of the singer's short life. The first one was released by Diane who then broke down in tears.

Not long afterwards, rain began to fall.

Aaliyah was buried at Ferncliff Cemetery and Mausoleum in Hartsdale, Westchester County, just outside of Manhattan. She was laid to rest beside her beloved grandmother.

Missy Elliott told me afterwards that, for her, the entire experience of Aaliyah's funeral felt other worldly. She was present, but she wasn't there. She could see all the stars, all the friends and family, but all she could think about was Aaliyah and all the fun times, all the creative moments they had experienced together. "What was going on in my mind while I was there?" said Elliott. "Actually I couldn't believe I was there. I would have rather believed that, when I walked out of there, that Aaliyah would have two-wayed me on the pager or something, you know what I'm saying? I just couldn't believe I was there. I wouldn't look at the casket, I wouldn't look at the carriage, any of that. I totally walked past it all. I was still in denial."

In fact, the day before the funeral, Elliott tried to contact Aaliyah on her pager. She knew, at that point, that Aaliyah was dead. She knew that there was nobody there to answer. But she had to check. She had to try. She wanted to hear Aaliyah's voice again, to talk about what was going on, to maybe chit-chat with her about the next project, the next song they could collaborate on. There was no answer on Aaliyah's pager. Elliott called her at home as well. Aaliyah wasn't there either. It took a few days to sink in, but Elliott finally realized the woman who had given her and Timbaland their first big chance was gone.

"I just talked to Aaliyah's mother the other day," Elliott told me in early October of 2001. "I continually pray for them that they have some peace of mind. When I see that they are at peace, it'll make me have a lot more peace with myself, because I know how close Aaliyah was to her mother, her father, and her brother. There wasn't nothing camouflage about their closeness as a family."

By October of 2001, the family had indeed begun the healing process. "At this time in the world a lot of people are in the same place," Rashad said in October 2001. "A lot of people from the tragedy on September 11—there are a lot of people in pain. We're not alone; none of us are alone. Right now is the time for everyone to just love each other and hold on." Jomo Hankerson, Aaliyah's cousin and the president of Blackground, said to me, "We've always dealt with crisis by making each other our pillars of strength. My aunt [Diane] and my dad [Barry] are very close and they absolutely have relied on each other throughout the whole ordeal. If anything, the family is closer and even tighter than before."

There will also be more Aaliyah music on the way, Jomo told me: "We always overcut our records—that was our A&R style. We always had more songs than we actually put on the record. We probably have between nine and twelve songs that are at various levels of completion but that do have Aaliyah's vocals. My dad and Aunt Diane have been talking about how we bring that to market. But we do have some material that we probably could make into a whole new record."

Jomo says the unreleased material largely consists of recently recorded songs. "I would say 75 percent of them are from the last two and a half years of her career," says Jomo. "Because this last album was really when Aaliyah came into full blossom creatively and so we worked with a lot of producers and cut a lot of records."

Something was lost, but something was gained. In the pop music world, women are often the creations of men. P. Diddy helped launch Faith Evans. Sony Records head Tommy Mottola helped engineer the career of Mariah Carey (her career hit a speed bump after she split with him). Celine Dion married her manager. Country singer Shania Twain married her songwriting partner and primary producer, Mutt Lange. Female vocalists—such as Whitney Houston and Celine Dion—are often not songwriters, and thus are open to the charge that they are merely interpreters of the works of male composers.

Aaliyah showed another path. She had begun her career as a seeming vessel for R.Kelly and had managed to break free to create her own identity. Her final movie, *The Queen of the Damned*, featured some hard rock music penned by Jonathan Davis of the group Korn. Aaliyah was open-minded enough that she was considering working with Davis on a remix of one or more of his hard-rocking songs. "She does really great, different stuff that's dark," Davis told MTV News. "She skirts the goth edge. There's something cool and mysterious about her. I dug that."

Aaliyah left behind a million might-have-beens. She might have worked with innovative folk rocker Beck on the Timbaland-produced cut "I Am Music." Beck did lay down some vocals for the song, but

Aaliyah wasn't in the studio at the time. Says Jomo, "Aaliyah and Beck, their schedules never coordinated. They were never in the studio at the same time. Beck laid down some parts with Timbaland that were going to be mixed into that song, but because they were never really in the studio to make it happen all at one time, it was going to be a cookie-cutter way we were putting the album together. I think if we did something with Beck in the future he's going to have to come in and do some new vocals to some of the stuff we have in the can."

Still, one version of "I Am Music" that features Aaliyah, Timbaland, and Static has been released. The elegiac song seems to embody music itself and the way it permeates life. Aaliyah only sings a brief part of the song herself, but it's a haunting cameo that sticks with the listener. It's almost as if she's slipped the bonds of earth and become music itself. It's one last glimpse at the elusive and adaptable nature of her talent. She could work with almost anybody, usually chose the best and most interesting people, and often took her art to new, even more intriguing places.

Aaliyah was also hoping, at some point, to collaborate with one of her musical heroes, Trent Reznor of Nine Inch Nails. Says Jomo: "They did get a chance to meet. They did not get a chance to work together. We were trying to get them together for [*Aaliyah*, her last album]. But Trent creatively is a very deliberate cat, and they were never able to coordinate schedules. And when Aaliyah's movie career took off it really made it hard for us to find the time and coordinate that with Trent. She was excited to meet him, and she told me afterwards that he was absolutely as incredible as she thought he would be when they met."

Aaliyah was building bridges: between hip-hop and R&B, between teen audiences and adult ones, between soul music and cutting-rock. With her death, that bridge tumbled into the abyss. Jermaine Dupri, one of Aaliyah's producers, said he was in his studio in Atlanta when he got the news about her death. "Somebody paged me," said Dupri. "I wanted to keep working and not believe it. That's the type of stuff you really don't want to believe. Couple of minutes later somebody else paged me and I'm like, 'Man, it's true.' "

Dupri says Aaliyah's voice, and her approach to singing, were part of what made her special: "Her voice was distinctive; off the top, when you heard it on the radio, you knew who it was. You separate yourself from a lot of people when you do that. There ain't many artists out there that have their own identity." Although she didn't write her own songs, she made them her own by investing them with her personality and by carefully choosing the partners she wished to work with. She was a young woman in control, calling the shots for her creative team, making decisions about her image, taking her career in new cinematic directions. I once asked her what the most important aspect of her work was and she didn't hesitate with her response. She said, "Being true to myself."

Now, she will always be that. The writer Joseph Conrad once captured the experience of being young and hungry for experience, the "romance of illusions" he called it, in a passage from his novella *Youth:* "But you here—you all had something out of life: money, love—whatever one gets on shore—and, tell me, wasn't that the best time, that time when we were young at sea, young and had nothing, on the sea that gives nothing, except hard knocks—and sometimes a chance to feel your strength—that only—what you regret?" Of course we don't want our favorite stars to die, of course we'd rather they stuck around and kept doing the things that they love and that we love—making quality movies or writing important books or recording great albums. But when stars do die young, it protects them. Their careers are forever sealed off from the compromises and corruptions of the world; they'll always remain immaculate, unsullied, pure. We'll never have to see Jimi Hendrix do a duet with Michael Bolton. We'll never have to suffer through the sight of Kurt Cobain dancing with Justin Timberlake. Dead stars are bright stars because they can never sell out. Of course we'd rather have them back. But, in a sad way, in death, they are truly ours forever. They are truly stars, up in the heavens, forever visible, forever out of reach. To paraphrase the words that Aaliyah once recited:

> Take her and cut her out in little stars,
> And she will make the face of heaven so fine
> That all the world will be in love with night
> And pay no worship to the garish sun